Waking

Up

As

Awareness

Waking Up As Awareness

Waking Up As Awareness

12 Simple Steps to Spontaneous Natural Meditation on Your True Self as Radiant Spacious Presence

By

Ramaji

Waking Up As Awareness

Books By Ramaji

The Spiritual Heart

No Mind No Problem

You Are Everything

The Tao of Non-Doing

Warning From Kali 2013

Waking Up As Awareness

Waking Up As Awareness

Copyright © Ramaji 2013

Ramaji.org

Ramaji Books
San Diego, California
Email: satsangwithramaji@gmail.com

This publication is presented to you for informational purposes only and is not a substitution for any professional advice. The contents herein are based on the views and opinions of the author.

What you do with this information is entirely your responsibility. If you do not agree with these terms, you may return this book for a full and prompt refund. Thank you.

All rights reserved. No part of this document may be reproduced or transmitted in any form, either by electronic or mechanical means including information storage and retrieval systems without the prior written permission of the publisher. The only exception is for a reviewer who may quote brief passages in the review.

Waking Up As Awareness

TABLE OF CONTENTS

JOURNEY TO THE HEART OF TRUTH

WHY ANOTHER BOOK ON SELF-INQUIRY MEDITATION?

12 SIMPLE STEPS ONE AT A TIME

STEP ONE: WHAT DO YOU KNOW ABOUT YOUR MIND?

STEP TWO: WHAT DO YOU KNOW ABOUT YOUR BODY?

STEP THREE: WHAT DO YOU KNOW ABOUT "WHO AM I"?

STEP FOUR: THE EFFORTLESS MORNING MEDITATION PRACTICE

EASY "WINDOW OF OPPORTUNITY" MORNING MEDITATION

Q&A: PRACTICAL POINTERS ON THE EFFORTLESS MEDITATION

STEP FIVE: THE SECRET OF THE MORNING MEDITATION PRACTICE

STEP SIX: IS THE WAKING STATE BASED ON THE PHYSICAL BODY?

STEP SEVEN: WHAT IS THE CONSCIOUS WAKING STATE?

STEP EIGHT: WHO IS IT EXACTLY THAT CLAIMS THE BODY?

STEP NINE: THE PRACTICAL TWO-STEP "WHO AM I?" MEDITATION

STEP TEN: HOW TO DO "WHO AM I?" MEDITATION DURING THE DAY

Q&A: SELF-INQUIRY MEDITATION WHEN DOING ACTIVITIES

STEP ELEVEN: PEACE NOW FROM THE "WHO AM I?" MEDITATION

Q&A: THE PEACE THAT RESULTS FROM THIS MEDITATION

STEP TWELVE: REVIEW, SUMMARY AND "WHAT COMES NEXT?"

THE 12 QUESTIONS AGAIN

SUMMARY OF WHAT WE COVERED

WHERE DO YOU GO FROM HERE?

RECOMMENDED READING

MEET THE AUTHOR

Waking Up As Awareness

JOURNEY TO THE HEART OF TRUTH

When I was 16 years old and living in a suburb of Los Angeles, California, I had a lucid dream that changed my life. In this dream, I was in India. I was with a yoga guru who spoke to me in Sanskrit. He took me through many hatha yoga postures, then I ended up sitting in padmasana, in lotus posture.

Then next thing that happened was literally mind-blowing. Everything exploded and my sense of separate self that I had been feeling in the dream dissolved totally and completely into a blissful peaceful Ocean of White Light.

When I woke up the next morning, my Kundalini was awakened. I also had amazing psychic powers. I'm not going to go into details, but I will say having this sudden unexpected Kundalini awakening was very difficult. It was hard enough just being a teenager. The extremes of emotion from the Kundalini were astonishing.

I managed to muddle my way through this crisis. I was in high school. I was still living with my parents. Though I knew next to nothing about yoga, meditation or Eastern religion, I knew enlightenment was real and that it was better than anything else.

I had a reading by a gifted spiritual psychic. She told me that I would have to wait a long time. She predicted that I would not see fruition of my spiritual yearnings until my 40s or 50s. She said I would have to be very patient.

It turned out she was right. To a teenager, waiting for the fulfillment of your heart's desire until you're 40 or so sounds like an eternity. Yet I sensed this delay was in my destiny.

What this experience did is force me to recalibrate everything in my inquisitive young life. Now life was transparent. It was just going through the motions. All the usual things that a young man could get excited about didn't amount to a hill of beans.

I had experienced a blissful transcendental Light that made everything else meaningless. All that life offered was now nonsense. Life was a cosmic joke, but I didn't know the punchline.

It was a paradoxical situation. It made me laugh. It made me cry. It made me doubt God. It made me love God. But one thing was for sure. I could never go back.

In the 1970s, I got involved with some marginal gurus. I made mistakes and I learned from them. I became a vegetarian. I started doing hatha yoga every morning.

In the early 1980s, I ended up living in a Sivananda ashram in Hollywood, California. It was there that my spiritual practice began to stabilize. The assistant head of the yoga center was studying Vipassana meditation. I learned about it from her.

I took up Vipassana ("Insight") meditation in earnest. I would meditate one or two hours a day plus practice mindfulness while walking and when I made tactile contract with something during the day out in the world.

The kind of Vipassana that I studied focused on fleeting body sensations. To be specific, on detecting the impermanence in these ever changing body sensations. This became possible when concentration was built up.

I had the good fortune to study with the Venerable Shinzen Young. He is a wonderful human being and a brilliant enlightened spiritual teacher. He has achieved much success as a meditation master. His success is well-deserved.

Even though he taught a more contemporary approach based on science, I was drawn to the classic Buddhist text *Vishuddimagga* (Path of Purification). I studied it and learned about the classical stages of the unfolding of impermanence. This traditional sequence of spiritual events or milestones on the road to Nibbana (Nirvana) is described by a few modern Vipassana teachers, too.

Even though I was living in a huge Western city, I went through these stages exactly as described in this book. These stages culminated precisely as the old book had predicted in the flash of Nirvana. I was doing walking meditation on a driveway in the back of the meditation retreat house in downtown Los Angeles when it happened.

Since Vipassana had been good to me, I stuck with it for seven years. But there came a time when it began to feel restrictive and limiting. There was not anything "wrong" with it. It is a brilliant practice. My clock of destiny was ticking. It was time to move on.

Advaita and Vipassana totally agree on the universal factor of impermanence as being key ("Anicca" in Pali). Vipassana is the Buddha's version of Self-inquiry meditation.

I was deep into my Vipassana meditation lifestyle when I met Kali at the Sri Ramakrishna Advaita Vedanta Temple in Hollywood, California. I was meditating there and the statue of Kali they keep up at the front moved. I saw Her walk by. Then I smelled the most lovely fragrance of sandalwood. Then She started talking to me.

Mother Kali has a very distinct way of talking. She talks like she is in total command, like she is the general and you are the private. She said to me, "You are mine. I own you. Your body is mine. I am in control of your destiny."

I was surprisingly at ease with the sudden turn of events. In my mind, I calmly replied "Okay, I believe you. If that is true, then what is next?"

Whispering in my ear again, Kali added "If you agree to this spiritual contract with me, then I will totally fulfill my side of the bargain. I can guarantee that you will attain spiritual liberation in this lifetime. You must be willing to surrender unconditionally to me from this point forward. Anything less than total surrender is unacceptable. If you comply, then I will control your life circumstances in order to guarantee your realization. But I cannot force this on you. You must choose it. What is your decision?"

I seriously doubt She said all of this. She is a Divine Mother of few words! But that is the essence of what She said to me. Without hesitation, I said "Yes. I surrender completely to you. I give my life over to you. My life is yours now."

She smiled. Then just as quickly as She had appeared, Her Presence was gone. When I asked somebody on the grounds about the Temple being open with the statue of Kali there, he acted surprised. The next time I visited the temple Her statue had been moved behind an iron fence. Kali in jail! I laughed out loud.

In early 1988, out of the blue the thought came to me that "My last name has the name of God, Ram, in it, so my guru is going to have Ram in his name." The thought just kept repeating over and over.

At this same time, I experienced a strange but not unpleasant metallic taste in the middle of my tongue. I have not felt that taste since. My impression is it was from Akasha (the etheric element).

A few months later I saw Ramesh's picture in a Hollywood paper. I instantly knew it was him. I intuitively knew with total certainty that meeting him was my destiny. He was going to change my life.

So what did I do? I decided to wait a year because I wanted to have one last year before I ran into the spiritual freight train called Ramesh! Looking back at it, it was a bizarre reaction. My thought at the time was "I'm not quite ready."

Fast forward to my encounter with Ramesh Balsekar in Solana Beach, October, 1989. I saw him later at several group meetings. This first time was at "Joe's Crab Shack" with about 50 people.

I have never loved a man like I loved him. I felt that he was my spiritual father. I love my biological father totally, yet the spiritual connection with Ramesh transcended everything. The feeling was like an ocean of love. I would cry and cry tears of joy.

The last event I went to took place in Pennsylvania, USA. I finally had a chance to talk to him one on one in a way. He was hanging out after giving a talk to the large group.

I walked rather timidly up to the small group that had gathered around him in the back of the room. He abruptly stopped talking to them and turned to me. I remember his penetrating gaze locking my eyes in place. There was no escaping those magnificent eyes!

I said something about how much I loved him and how I wanted to come to India to be his servant. He looked genuinely shocked.

"Oh, no," he said, "that is nonsense! You should not be lingering around. I have given you everything I can give you. Go study with other teachers if you like. Or just do whatever you want. It won't matter. I have given you everything. Now you must move on with your life. I cannot help you anymore."

I said "Thank you" and reached out to give him a hug, which he accepted. The joy and gratitude you feel with the person who has revealed the Self to you simply cannot be described. So even though this was the last thing I wanted to hear, I intuitively knew he was right. I never saw him again. He lives on in my heart and in my life.

My journey then took me back to Sri Nisargadatta Maharaj and Sri Ramana Maharshi. I studied their teachings all over again and practiced the unique meditations they taught. In 2006, Kundalini completed Her journey to the Crown chakra. A passageway from the Crown down to the Heart on the right called Amrita Nadi was revealed to me.

There was a life-transforming flash of Amrita Nadi. It was the ultimate spiritual event of my life. Amrita Nadi ("channel of immortality") and Hridayam (the causal Heart on the right side of the chest) are talked about by Sri Ramana Maharshi.

The awakening of Amrita Nadi has been described as "the light of a thousand suns." The world turns translucent and disappears in a blaze of Divine Light.

When the world returns, it is not the same world. That world is gone forever. There is only the one supreme Self. You can still perceive the world and function in the world, but for you the world is literally the universal Self.

I have come full circle. The Light that was revealed in 1966 was the Light that was realized in 2006. In 2012, I moved to San Diego and began giving public Satsang.

Many Blessings in the One Supreme Self, Ramaji

Waking Up As Awareness

WHY ANOTHER BOOK ON SELF-INQUIRY MEDITATION?

Because of the avalanche of information about meditation, there is considerable confusion as to what are the best methods for attaining enlightenment or Self-realization. If you yearn to reach the highest state of awareness and freedom, you will benefit from understanding the "Who am I?" or Self-inquiry meditation.

One of the very greatest spiritual teachers and meditation masters of all time was Sri Ramana Maharshi. There are many today who are still influenced by beloved Ramana and feel blessed by his Presence. This includes myself.

It is on the basis of that sacred connection that I have taken on this project of explaining the "Who am I?" or Self-inquiry meditation in the most practical, straightforward "how to" manner possible. My inspiration for this approach is also the teachings of Sri Sadhu Om Swamigal. This Self-realized disciple of Sri Ramana Maharshi became known as an expert on Ramana's Self-inquiry method.

My position is that a spiritual student should do the kind of meditation that he enjoys and feels naturally attracted to. We are able to maintain our meditation because we love it.

If we do not feel a passionate love for it, or something similar, whatever it means for the student, then the motivation will not be there. Sooner or later, the meditation will be dropped. For me, meditation has been a life-long love affair.

I suspect making this commitment to meditation is even more challenging today where every week there are new technological toys and other civilized distractions offered to the public. In some ways, those who lived back when nature dominated had it easier. If you have spent time camping in the deep woods or similar, then you have experienced the silence that is one of nature's most precious gifts.

On the other hand, today very secret and sacred information is out in the open for all to use and apply. It is explained very directly. So perhaps it all balances out!

Although I talk about "12 steps to spiritual enlightenment" and reading one step a day, I have no illusions that attaining Self-realization takes just a few weeks!

While I would not put it outside the realm of possibility, as anything is possible for the Self, the concept of the book is that the reader will have gained a solid and reliable foundation for a lifetime of rewarding practice in the "Who am I?" meditation.

Once the goal is achieved, then the meditation falls away by itself. If "Who am I?" meditation is bringing the meditator deep joy and ever deepening peace and release, then he or she should stay with it until they gain Self-realization.

It is a tremendous boon to receive this meditation and have the time and good health for practicing it. These precious advantages need to be utitilzed to their fullest.

Since the reader is already the Self, it is also accurate to say that when realization takes place, it does so with the speed of a lightning flash. After all, how long does it take to realize what you already are?

Not long, obviously, when the actual realization takes place. So 12 days is plenty, as even 12 seconds would be way longer than the actual "time" required for something to take place that completely transcends both time and space.

Frankly, even a split second would be too long for something to occur that has, quite literally, ALREADY occurred. You just don't (apparently) know it!

I assert that in your Heart of hearts, you do know that it is true -- and that is why you are reading this right now. At some level, YOU KNOW You Are the SELF!

There is no doubt for me that "Who am I?" is the ultimate enlightenment meditation technique. However, it seems that many people find it difficult to do. This is in part because its practical application has been poorly explained.

Sri Ramana Maharshi has explained everything quite clearly, as have some of his disciples. You will find a Recommended Reading list at the end of this book.

I believe that after reading this "12 Steps to Spiritual Enlightenment" book you will find it easier to understand the teachings of Ramana and his main disciples.

Due to the differences in culture, language and religious upbringing, sometimes their insights sound strange. I have done my best to "Westernize" the "Who am I?" meditation and its key ingredients to help modern meditators in the West.

The books I recommend are the ones that I personally used in my sadhana, so the fact that I put them here means that I believe they are totally on the mark. They are of enormous practical value in terms of helping you understand exactly how to do this special meditation technique and what the results might be like for you.

I take full responsibility for the words that follow. I purposefully did not insert quotations from Sri Ramana Maharshi to "back up" my practical points and insights. This original material must stand on its own.

While I believe that my advice and overall message are in complete alignment with what Ramana really taught, my words must do their own work. Those who are able to have success with Ramana's remarkable meditation based upon my practice pointers will be all the proof I could ever need or want.

With Blessings in the One Supreme Self, Ramaji
San Diego, California
Ramaji.org

12 SIMPLE STEPS ONE AT A TIME

Since this information is concentrated, you may want to consider reading this book literally one day at a time. The idea is that there is something to do each day.

You are given plenty to absorb. In this time of technology-induced adult ADD, it may be a good idea to read just one chapter, one day, one step. Take it in slowly. Gradually absorb the insights. The result will be inspiration and upliftment.

Then you may find that chapter of the day rising in your mind as a contemplation. You may ruminate about it during the day, which is good. Whatever calls your mind back to the Self, to the precious Silence and pure feeling of Being, is good.

Even if you do rush through the book, and read all 12 steps in one or a few sittings, I think you will probably want to come back to some of it in order to fully absorb what is being presented.

The only real burden is the mind, which is just a bundle of thoughts. Even the weight and pressure from the so-called "world" and so-called "other people," which may seem so real now, is really just thoughts. Central to this whole charade is the I-thought or "I am the body" thought who is behind this hypnotic illusion.

Through the dedicated application of the "Who am I?" meditation (Self-inquiry), the truth of this "scam" will get exposed. Then it all comes tumbling down like a house of cards. But you will not have to wait for an increase of peace. You will quickly experience a life-changing reduction in stress as the thoughts drop off.

I wrote this book because, to my knowledge, there is nothing else like it. The book by Sri Sadhu Om Swamigal, cited in the back, was my inspiration. It is the only other book I know of which speaks so directly and plainly about HOW TO do this meditation. While there is no one "right" way, rest assured that this way works!

After you have gone through this guide, I suggest reading his book. At the time of this writing, you can purchase it online if you want the physical book or you can download it for free as a pdf ebook. Michael James, the translator of the original Tamil and copyright holder, is making it available. All the details are in the back.

In case it is important to you that teachings be shown to be directly supported by the words of Ramana, he has referenced many quotations from Sri Ramana Maharshi to explain and support the details of this highly practical approach.

When I was first doing Self-inquiry or "Who am I?" meditation, I would really liked to have had access to a book like this. With this idea as my inspiration, I have made it available to you now. It has been a labor of love. It brings me great joy to share it.

Waking Up As Awareness

STEP ONE: WHAT DO YOU KNOW ABOUT YOUR MIND?

This is a practical self-help course in 12 short steps, so let's get going. Let's find out what you understand about your mind.

Please write down your answers to the following questions. Or you can just think about it.

I would prefer that you write your answers down and put a date on the paper. In fact, it might be a good idea to keep a journal to keep track of your progress.

The reason for this is at the end of this book I am going to ask you the same exact questions. I fully expect that your replies will show a radical transformation.

So if you don't mind, please take just a few minutes to write down your answers to these crucial questions. Please note that I am NOT providing the "answers" at the back of the book or any such thing.

This book you are reading IS the answers to these questions. That is why I fully expect that by the end of the book, after you have read it and applied it to some extent, your answers will, at the very least, be more confident and clear.

By the way, everything that you need to know in order to "get enlightened" or attain Self-realization is in this book. At the same time, I have provided a short Recommended Reading list.

This is because (a) I want you to read the words of Sri Ramana Maharshi directly and (b) the way another author says the same useful point can strike you differently because he said it differently. I just would like you to have every possible advantage on your journey to realize your true Self.

(1) What is the mind?

(2) What is the I-thought?

(3) What is the "I am the body" idea?

(4) What prevents you from being fully enlightened or Self-realized?

STEP TWO: WHAT DO YOU KNOW ABOUT YOUR BODY?

The writing down part here at the beginning has two more steps.

As I said before, I would prefer that you actually write down your thoughts and understanding on a piece of paper and then put a date on it. Thanks.

Even if you do not gain at least a taste of enlightenment soon after reading this book and applying its instructions, I sincerely believe that you will understand what it is that is preventing you from that Self-realization. We can thank Sri Ramana Maharshi for stating these secrets so openly and with such spiritual force.

(1) Where is the mind?

(2) Where is the I-thought?

(3) Where is the "I am the body" idea?

(4) In relationship to your physical body, what is the location or identity or nature of what prevents you from being fully enlightened or Self-realized?

Waking Up As Awareness

STEP THREE: WHAT DO YOU KNOW ABOUT "WHO AM I"?

This is the third and last step where I will be discussing theory and asking you to write your answers down. Please make the effort, even if your answers are short.

Very soon we get into the concrete real life practice of the highly effective "Who am I?" meditation. As I said before, I believe this is the ultimate meditation.

But first, you do want to get a handle on why exactly you are wanting to do "Who am I?" or Self-inquiry meditation. So please think about that for a moment.

The other thing to have in place before we get started is a good understanding of why exactly does this question "Who am I?" arise in the first place.

After all, Sri Ramana Maharshi did not invent the question!

"Who am I?" already existed long before Ramana formulated it as a meditation method. Some would even say it is not a method at all, it is just the question of life, something to be asked naturally and spontaneously.

The reason "Who am I?" arises, whether or not you are doing it as a form of meditation, is that the real "I," which is Awareness, has found itself confined.

To be even more specific, the true "I" finds itself strangely localized and, therefore, feels profoundly limited.

"Who am I?" does not arise in Awareness itself. The question arises in the mind. It is the mind that asks this question. Awareness already knows who and what it is.

The mind asks this question because it exists and it has a sense of its existence as being concrete, localized and separate. So when the mind asks "Who am I?" you could say it is really asking "How did I end up here? How is it that I am concrete, localized and separate?"

Awareness, the Self, is naturally unbounded and unlimited. It has no sense of limitation of any kind. In everyday terms, this means it is NOT stuck in Time and it is NOT localized in Space. It is prior to and beyond both Time and Space.

So here I would like you to answer these questions. I prefer that you write it down and put a date on your answer, perhaps in a new meditation journal.

(1) Why do YOU want to do "Who am I?" or Self-inquiry meditation?

(2) Why or how does this question "Who am I?" naturally arise in the first place?

(3) Why is it that the mind asks this question but Awareness does not?

(4) Who exactly is asking this ultimate Big Question "Who am I?"

STEP FOUR: THE EFFORTLESS MORNING MEDITATION PRACTICE

If you find this effortless special morning meditation practice useful, then it would be a good idea to incorporate it in your life and do it every day. Once you have even a little bit of success with it, I think you will be hooked!

There is a very special window of opportunity that arises right when you are waking up. This spiritual opportunity is even more amazing as it is effortless.

You are, of course, already the Self, your enlightened nature, right now.

Naturally, a question that then arises is "If that is true, then why am I not experiencing that today?"

The answer has two parts.

One: In fact, you do have moments within the 24 hour cycle of day and night where you are resting in the Self, in yourself as natural Awareness.

Two: Of these moments, there is a special moment that arises right before you awaken fully into the physical world. I call it "special" because it is a between time. You are between sleep and waking.

It is "special" because it is relatively easy to access and experience. Also because it is totally effortless. You could say that "the veil is thinned" at that moment.

However, this special window of opportunity usually comes and goes very quickly. For this reason, it is generally not noticed by people.

Any spiritual practice that you are already doing will enhance your ability to access this special window that opens at the time you wake up into this world.

For that reason, I can honestly say that if you really love whatever that practice is and you do not want to give it up, but just want to take something very useful from this book, then I would say the thing to take is this secret effortless meditation.

Now I am not going to give you an explanation as I want you to discover it and experience it for yourself. If you have already read my detailed explanation in my other books or from another source, such as Sri Sadhu Om, then you have those words and ideas.

However, such book knowledge is no substitute for direct experience. You must still DO the practice if you are to benefit from it!

So even though it is truly effortless, you must still remember to do it.

Please note that the practice of keeping the body still when you just wake up will increase your recall of dreams. While working with dreams is not a part of this practice, improved dream recall may be a beneficial side-effect of doing it.

However, please do the practice as described. If after you have done the practice, you wish to record your dreams, that is fine. For some people, there may be a good way to blend the two practices to enhance them, but I do not know what that is.

Waking Up As Awareness

EASY "WINDOW OF OPPORTUNITY" MORNING MEDITATION

(1) THE VERY INSTANT that you wake up from sleeping, DO NOT MOVE.

(2) This is very important: Do NOT move your physical body.

(3) Now ask yourself a question like one of the following.

Or silently and intuitively feel and sense the truth of the situation. Or you may see something with your spiritual vision that answers the question for you. Or possibly an insight, in words or a thought or a sound, will just come to you out of the blue.

"Where is the I?"

"What is the I?"

"Who am I?"

"Is the body who I am?"

"Am I the physical body?"

"Where did I just come from?"

"Where am I?"

(4) If you have the time, continue to lay there contemplating the space you are in.

(5) If possible, allow half an hour to very slowly and gradually enter into the world. Do not do the meditation for a minute or two and then jump up and rush around. Ideally, you will ease into this world, paying full attention as you do so.

I don't mean you have to lay there for half an hour, although that is an option. If you are an active person, then I am suggesting that you lay quietly in bed for five or 10 minutes. Then sit in meditation in your usual place for up to 20 minutes.

As you ease into your day, move slowly and mindfully. Do your best to remember and stay in the lightness and peace of the morning "gap." If you have to go to work, then adjust the minutes accordingly, and schedule a short time period right after you get up where you stay in total silence with NO interruptions.

This period of time when you wake up and right after is the most precious time of the day. This is your "me" time (your true "I" time). Even if you have to go to work, every day have at least 10 minutes right after you wake up all to yourself.

You are fresh from exposure to the thought-free Self, your true identity. Honor this precious time. It will set a beautiful positive expansive tone for your whole day.

The Self is "you," just without limitations. It is like you have been walking around in a suit of heavy armor. When the armor finally comes off for good, you feel that a great weight has been lifted. You feel free of all of those limitations.

But you still feel like "you." So don't worry. You have everything to gain and nothing to lose. Whatever you will "lose" was false and only creating big problems for you!

This first 10 minutes to half an hour in the morning, as much as you can spare daily, is crucial because it is time where you are "fresh" and the world has not yet invaded you. When you start obsessively thinking-thinking about the world and other people, then you have lost this special window. The "gap" is closed.

By remaining in the Self, in the sacred silence, right after you wake up, you are able to dwell in your pure identity unencumbered by thoughts. When thoughts about others and the world start rising up fast and furious, especially thoughts about problems, then you are in the world. You may still be at home sitting in meditation, but your mind is fully reactivated. The result is unnecessary suffering.

What I am saying is do your best to preserve the pristine Silence that you came out of when you woke up. This natural Awareness state has no thoughts in it. It is the real deal. By staying quiet right after getting out of bed, you can extend the "gap" of sacred silence and openness that is the Self and abide in it in sitting meditation.

(6) Be profoundly aware of the transition, the gap, between the dream or sleeping state and the so-called waking state thought to be associated with the body. If you observe very closely, you will see that just before you as the mind enter into the body to claim it, you have an experience of yourself as the Light of Awareness.

(7) Once you have "grasped" this Light of Awareness for even a strong firm instant, meaning you have seen it, felt it or otherwise witnessed it and validated its arising, then you dedicate yourself to extending this subjective window where the Self or Light is making itself known. Having seen the Light, you embrace it.

This is how you can blend the deep sleep state in which the Self resides with the conventional waking state without trying to access the deep sleep state while the physical body is asleep. Just as the morning twilight, the Brahma Murta, partakes of both the night or self-luminosity and the day, the solar blast that makes the physical visible, so your private twilight as you wake up from sleep mixes both the divine spiritual Light and the conventional waking state.

This unconditioned divine revelation takes place prior to the actual arising of the fully embodied state where the body-identification is firmly locked in place.

This "spiritual intervention" prior to the I-thought falsely claiming the physical body as its own self and property is an unprecedented opportunity to receive the grace-drenched full "darshan" or holy vision of the authentic supreme Self!

As you mix the third ingredient, which is the conscious awareness into the twilight blend of the private Brahma Murta, you will begin to awaken to That which you already are now. No longer will this be concepts. You will taste the peace yourself.

Waking Up As Awareness

Q&A: PRACTICAL POINTERS ON THE EFFORTLESS MEDITATION

Q: What if I don't see or experience anything? Am I just wasting my time then?

A: There is no more important time of your day than this moment when you wake up. Even if we look at it in terms of just reducing stress and having more happiness, it is very important.

The way that you wake up sets the tone for the rest of your day. If you wake up slowly and allow yourself to appreciate the finer points of being alive, of being reborn on a fresh new day, this gives you a kind of positive psychological opening or opportunity. You can feel how this day really is new, meaning that there are wonderful new possibilities waiting for you.

Q: Are there other benefits to doing this practice of lying still when you just wake up?

A: Like any other practice, it is a noble suggestion. If you just lie there and it means nothing to you, then there is no reason to do it. But if you resonate with this approach, then at the very least you will gain better recall of your dreams. You will access details that you had forgotten.

The other thing you may experience is that even if you do not catch the flash of the Self as it happened while you were waking up, if you lie in bed in contemplation, you will be able to do a review of the "events" of your waking up.

In this review, you may actually find that you did experience the Light of the Self, only you did not remember it or you did not know what it was. Awareness, however, was present.

Q: What about keeping my cell phone near my bed? I do that and so do lots of other people.

A: I think you know my answer. I know this is what people do nowadays. I would not have the cell phone or computer close to you like that. Then one of your first thoughts will be to check in with your friends or with world events or the stock market via your cell or laptop.

This all sounds innocent enough, and it is a wonder of modern technology. Now we can all be "connected." The problem from the standpoint of meditation, especially a meditation that you do right when you wake up, is that the so-called "world" really is nothing other than your thoughts.

The "world" that seems to be "out there" does not appear in this three-dimensional apparently solid form for you until AFTER the I-thought has completed its morning task of claiming and taking over the body. If your awareness is subtle enough, then you will see the I-thought go to the head, take the brain over, and then take the whole body over via the nervous system.

After it has conquered the body, you could say then it conquers the world. It does not actually conquer the world, as the world is the Self, but it creates an effective illusion of doing so.

If you did not catch its magic trick of taking over the body, then you will not catch its magic trick of projecting the illusion of a three-dimensional world filled with busy people running around doing a bunch of stuff. The world is fascinating, but the world is not real the way we think it is.

Q: So you are saying that by becoming more aware of the waking up process, we can also become more aware of what the world really is and how to become free of it?

A: Yes. The whole "reincarnation" thing that you do each morning is not complete until the world as you know it is recreated as well. After the I-thought has taken over the brain and the body, it then projects a dark film over the eyes from within the brain.

Since people are already identified with the body, they are looking outward and think this is the only direction to look. The I-thought does not need to literally create the world. All it needs to do is color and twist our PERCEPTION of the world. It does this by creating a subtle yet dense and highly effective FILTER through which you look, hear and experience with your senses.

You think that you are seeing the world as it is, but in fact you are looking at the world through a filter that the "I am the body" thought created in order to keep you deceived. After all, now that it has taken over the body, is it just going to lay around like somebody in a coma? Of course not.

You can think of this perception altering filter as being like wearing dark glasses that change everything you see and experience. You don't know you are wearing trick glasses.

Then when you take the dark glasses off, you are suddenly startled by the brightness and beauty and perfection of this so-called "world." What these glasses were limiting you to was very grimy and narrow and confining. Since the true world is actually the Self, it is glorious.

Frankly, these dark glasses, this I-thought perception filter, makes everything "outside" of you look dingy, dark, grim and depressing. It makes you feel small, worthless and helpless in contrast to a big bad ugly world that is "out there." This world seems powerful, yet it makes no sense!

This is the cold cruel crazy world of the I-thought. It looks like a gray foreboding prison planet, but it is all a clever sophisticated illusion to keep us confused, weak, sad and submissive.

The real world, the world of the Self, is close to the beautiful heaven or paradise that children live in or religions talk about. There is love everywhere. It is better than the fantasies.

There is only joy and peace. In place of darkness and suffering, there are rainbows and smiling faces. The world of the Self is the real world. There is freedom for all and always a celebration.

Q: So you are saying the real risk of thinking right away of the world and our involvement in it is that we will be sucked into this sophisticated three-dimensional illusion and not even know it?

A: Yes. Your spiritual goal is to dwell in the morning gap as pure Awareness. That will never happen if you're already thinking about the Internet or Facebook or Twitter or LinkedIn or whatever the instant you wake up. You blew right pass your opportunity to discover the gap.

At first, what you see in the effortless Morning Meditation may seem like just a tiny light, a little glimmer. That is a glimpse of the Self. As it expands, it is the Light that overcomes the world.

There is a subtle trap here that even many people who meditate do not notice. If you are thinking or assuming that the world is "real," implied in that belief is the assumption that "I am the body."

The hypnosis of "I am the body" must arise first before you can have the hypnosis of the world.

These concepts of "The world is out there" and "The world out there is real" and "That world out there is real and filled with a whole lot of other people like me all doing a bunch of stuff" all follow from believing that this experience "I am this physical body" is real.

The implication is that if you can become more alert to the process of how you become identified with the body, then not only are you freeing yourself from that identification, you have set in motion a sequence of events in awareness where you will be setting yourself free from the icy grip of a cold uncaring world that seems full of suffering. You are setting yourself free from this dark three-dimensional distortion that makes our heaven on earth look like a grim dingy jail.

As your realization of the Self deepens, the burden of the so-called world lifts. The need for a spiritual person to remove themselves from the world in order to meditate or be free from it disappears. It is seen that the world is none other than the Self. Everything is the Self.

So the phony three-dimensional physical world of the I-thought is just additional layers of thought and hypnosis. This phony prison world is the icing on the cake for the I-thought.

I don't know if you have ever seen a stage hypnotist bring a bunch of people up on the stage and make them act like chickens or cows or other funny things. I saw somebody do that in Las Vegas and it was quite amazing -- and very funny!

Well, this stage hypnotist comedian had nothing on the I-thought. The I-thought is the master hypnotist of the world. The stage hypnotist gets people to think they are chickens. The I-thought gets the spiritual Beingness to think it is a limited physical body.

But does the stage hypnotist stop there? No, he is just getting warmed up!

He then gets people to stand up and walk around and cluck like a chicken. He makes them interact with other people who are also hypnotized. It is hilarious because we know that these are really people and not animals. But for the impact to be the maximum, we have to see the hypnotized subject acting like a chicken, clucking, scratching the ground and so on.

Likewise, the I-thought is not content merely to take over the body. The world is its stage, so it then gets people to interact with other people. Then it all seems so very real. We are all doing it, we are all believing it, we are all interacting with each other as if it is real, and so on.

But it isn't. The world is a stage and those who are not aware have become chickens instead of the human beings that they are. They can cluck and scratch all day long, but they are still human and it is still all just hypnosis. It all takes place on an imaginary stage. It is not real.

Q: Can you talk about how you discovered this spiritual gap where the Light of Awareness shows up in the morning when you wake up?

A: I received the clue from Sri Sadhu Om Swamigal from his book. The details about how to get his book are in the back. I cannot recommend his book strongly enough. It is fantastic.

When I first began my investigation, I was coming from a background where I had experienced astral projection. So I was expecting that the astral or dream body would just get "sucked into" or drawn into the physical body somehow. I had experienced a suction type thing when returning to the body from an astral projection, so that was my expectation.

But as I studied the sequence of events that occur in consciousness when waking up, I realized that I was wrong. The gap between the astral or dream universe and the waking or physical universe is huge. They are two totally distinct environments. They are very different.

I realized that even though I had astral traveled and had been conscious in the astral body, I was still convinced that I was the physical body. I had not challenged that assumption. So when I was returning to the body from my astral projection, I did not examine the process. I just got sucked back into the physical as the physical body was "who I am."

But when I stopped making that assumption and looked for the gap instead of looking forward to the physical body as my final and "real" destination, I found the gap. As I explored this gap, it got bigger and more interesting. I found that I could dwell in this morning gap. I discovered the spontaneous display of the Self, of the unbounded self-luminous Awareness, in this gap.

This helped me enormously to weaken the hold of the I-thought on this body. I was able to see for myself all of the things I have talked about. I saw directly for myself how the I-thought shoots up to the brain, takes over the body and then creates a phony and distorted world.

After you see all of this, the Self must still come forward so that you realize the Self and the world as the Self. But once you have observed these details for yourself, I would say that the jig is up. The hypnotic game of the "I am the body" thought has been exposed for good.

Q: I wake up very groggy. I do not have the problem of waking up right away and instantly thinking of the world and other people. My brain feels very fuzzy.

A: That is actually a good thing. The grogginess is a sign of sleeping deeply, and sleeping deeply is very good. The best thing is to go very slow. Do not try to impose waking upon that state.

Lie still and be available to that groggy state. You will find that it is a valuable defense against the world. The world is just thoughts. In your groggy state, these thoughts that make the world seem so real are having trouble formulating themselves. This is very positive.

What people don't realize is that the so-called world is in fact a terrible imposition upon them. It is like an invading force. Because they think the world is this great big thing that holds all the possibilities, they surrender to it and let it boss them around.

But as you get know your true Self better, as you explore and discover the precious gold that lies hidden within your humble first person identity feeling, you discover a grand feeling of having a royal identity. Your sense of inner nobility and of your supreme self-worth expands and evolves.

At some point, you see that the world depends on you, not the other way around. That is when you see this deal that you have made with the world is not a good trade. It is like you have a bag of gold. Thinking that your gold is worthless dirt, you trade a million in gold for a loaf of bread.

You made the trade because you were hungry. But really it was because you did not know the value of the gold you already had in your hand.

Once you realize that your first person identity feeling is pure gold, that it is the basis for everything else, that it is like a compass pointing to the true nature of the Self, then the joy of your great adventure of Self-discovery takes over.

We human beings want to feel good. All good feelings come from the Self, the Heart.

Q: You use the language that "the Self comes forward." What do you mean exactly?

A: Obviously, the Self does not really come forward. But it may seem that way. In fact, the Self is in the gap already. Or you could say the Self, the luminous Awareness, IS the gap.

The Self seems to come forward as before it seemed to be hidden. It is all due to the power of attention. Now that you have focused your attention here in the gap, you will see all kinds of things that you did not see before.

Since we think that our lives are lived during the day after waking up, and the night is just dreams, that makes our day very important. The most important part of our day is waking up, and the most important part of waking up is to find out "Who exactly is waking up?"

Who is this "I" that thinks it is waking up from dreams in sleep and becoming the body?

So the effortless Morning Meditation is simply another form of asking the question "Who am I?"

STEP FIVE: THE SECRET OF THE MORNING MEDITATION PRACTICE

It is my preference that you do the effortless special Morning Meditation practice at least one time before you read this step. Then you will have experience to add meaning to the words. If you want to go ahead and read it, that's fine, though.

My guess is that you would like to know exactly why you are not supposed to move your physical body when you wake up. I will explain that right now.

If you start moving your physical body the moment you wake up and start doing something, this is like saying "I am my physical body." In the easy secret Morning Meditation you first discover that there is a "gap" and then rest in this "gap." This "gap" naturally occurs as you are emerging from sleep.

So you don't move your body. Instead, you remain very still and make it a meditation. You investigate with your calm clear awareness this fresh dawn-type space of just waking up in the morning. You want to know "How exactly do I become my body at this time?"

It is like you are waiting in the morning darkness or twilight. You are waiting for the sun to come up. You don't want to miss any detail. So you are watching and waiting, studying the horizon so that you can catch the very first glimpse of the sun coming up over the mountains. If you wait until the sun has risen and it is overhead, then you will have missed the "rising" of the sun entirely.

This "gap" where the sun is rising, the sunrise, is very different from the sun when it is up in the sky. There many nuances to observe as the morning changes from dark to twilight to the sun peaking over the mountains to it rising up in the sky.

Also, it is better if you don't have your cell phone right next to you. Avoid other distractions in the bedroom like the television or computer. These technologies represent the world. In this case, they are the world invading your holy temple.

You should think of your bedroom as a place of meditation, as a sacred place, a temple. It is where you "die" at night, so to speak. The next day, in the morning, it is where you take "rebirth" as the physical body.

It may sound extreme to say that you die at night or whenever you go to bed and then when you wake up it is like you have reincarnated, but it is more true than most of us realize. You were actually residing in other bodies as you slept, in the astral and causal bodies and in their respective dimensions.

"You" were not in this physical body of yours at all. "You" were gone and living in other dimensions. Some people call those other dimensions "heaven."

Here is what happens when you wake up in the morning. It may seem like you just woke up from a dream or some kind of unconscious sleep state. Or you may not remember a dream at all. You just wake up and think you are the body.

In fact, the reality is just very different. If that is all that you are noticing, then you are missing a most important step that is IN BETWEEN sleeping and waking.

Just before you wake up into being your physical body in this physical world, there is an intervention by the Self, the pure Awareness, your already enlightened Self. The Self literally appears and manifests itself in all of its pristine shining glory the instant just before you wake up.

Even if you were in a dream just before you woke up, so that your experience seems to be that you just "woke up from a dream," that is not completely accurate.

The more accurate explanation is that you were dreaming and then, just before you woke up into this apparent physical world, you accessed the pure equivalent of the deep sleep state (the Self). Lucid Awareness arises just before entering the body.

The point of the effortless "waking up" Morning Meditation practice is to widen the window of opportunity at this very special moment in the morning where the lucidity of the Self or self-luminous pure Awareness makes itself known. As you have no doubt realized by now, if you wait until you feel fully identified with the physical body, the process of accessing the Aware Self is neither easy nor direct.

For this reason, some people meditate for hours a day. They are trying to storm the Kingdom of Heaven via will or effort. That is fine, as it is a strong spiritual action, but any meditator would be wise to incorporate this easy Morning Meditation.

The conventional outline of the sleeping process is that we fall asleep, we spend some time in the deep sleep state, we spend some time in the dream state, and then we wake up. There is alternation between the states and so forth, but the essence of the model is that during the night we first go the deepest that we can go, into the deep sleep. Later in the sleeping process, we are at the lighter level called dreams.

My reason for describing this conventional model is that it is not quite accurate. It makes it sounds like the only time that you could possibly access the Self via the deep sleep state is in the middle of deep sleep, which is quite difficult. By definition, there is no ego consciousness in the deep sleep state.

Nonetheless, as Sri Ramana Maharshi pointed out, the sadhana of true enlightenment or Self-realization is, in essence, the bringing of the organic deep sleep state with its naturally restful peace, bliss and contented fullness into the waking state. In other words, the goal is to make the deep sleep state conscious.

You do not have to invent enlightenment or create the deep sleep state. It already exists. You also do not have to invent your waking or conscious awareness state. You are already in that state during the course of your day.

What we have then, as a spiritual asset for our earnest quest, is a natural deep sleep state that appears to be submerged in a kind of mysterious unconsciousness. We also have the precious spiritual asset handed to us as a gift by life of the natural waking state that all normal human beings, the six billion or so of us, share.

In contrast to the exotic deep sleep state, the conscious waking state of the average human being seems mundane, plain, unremarkable, even trivial or problematic.

We could say that the superficial person lives just in this waking state. So they are obsessed with popular culture, with fashion and music trends, and with clothing and beautifying their body. Perhaps they are preoccupied with money or power. What they know is that they are the body in the world, and that is pretty much it.

However, there are many problems associated with this superficial approach to the waking state. As a result, some people try to go "deeper" into their self. The direction that people often go is into dreams, visions, symbols and other types of meditation that are related to the dream state.

From this we get the expression "to realize your dreams." If your goal is to realize your dreams, that makes dreams more important than waking life!

As the inquiry or search continues, sooner or later you bump up against the fact that the dream state itself has to come from something. In other words, you start to ask the question "Where does this dream state come from? What is the source of the dream state experience?"

The answer is pretty obvious. The dream state emerges out of the deep sleep state.

That is where we run into the problem!

Yes, it is fairly easy to access dreams and even become conscious and awake within them while still sleeping, but then what?

A few rare people have been able to transition from being conscious in dreaming into being conscious in a way in the deep sleep state. As far as I know, this is not a path that the average meditator will be able to follow with any reliability.

According to the popular scientific model, when we fall asleep at night we go from the most superficial state, the waking state, into a state that is in between waking and sleeping, then down into a deep sleep state, and then back up into a dreaming state (REM sleep). This cycle repeats itself during the night.

The priority for the body is first to spend time in the dark healing depths of deep sleep. As the night progresses, we start spending more time in the dream state (REM sleep). We do not return to the depths of the deep sleep state. That is why when we wake up we may have the experience of waking up "from a dream."

I realize this is an over-simplification, but I am keeping it simple to illustrate an important point. This scientific model is saying that our only access to deep sleep was early in the sleep cycle and we cannot access it at the time of waking up.

If we embrace this model, we now have a BIG problem. Our ability to be conscious appears to be restricted to waking and dreaming. There is also the transition between the waking state and falling asleep, the in-between or twilight state, that some people call "hypnogogic." It is like a natural trance state.

The bottom line is that now, having bumped into the apparently pitch black dark and inaccessible deep sleep state, the ordinary person turns away and just continues to explore dreaming and waking states. Unfortunately, since the Self or Awareness can be said to reside in or behind the peaceful deep sleep state, they have also turned away from the most direct access to the Self, their real nature.

The solution to the dilemma of the "Do Not Enter" message that people encounter when trying to work with the deep sleep state is the secret Morning Meditation.

The effortless Morning Meditation practice is based on the insight that the Self gracefully appears JUST BEFORE you "wake up" into the state where you claim the physical body as yourself. You then find yourself in the typical waking state where you feel like a struggling "doer" in the physical world.

Therefore, you have an extraordinary opportunity right at the precise instant you are waking up! You can claim the Self as your true self, not the physical body!

In that in-between state, that gap that has dreaming on one side and the conscious waking state on the other, the Self briefly flashes and makes its Presence known. This is the "no mind" or "only don't know" state.

Serious meditators may be aware that the best time to meditate for most people is early in the morning. In the Hindu tradition, there is what is called "Brahma Murta," meaning "the hour of God."

The idea is to rise up in the pre-dawn hours just before or just when the sun is coming up. Then you meditate.

If things go quite well during this dawn twilight time, then you may become aware of how you are emerging into this physical manifestation, of how you are taking incarnation.

If you had to produce a rule for everybody to follow, then this is superb advice. Be up at this time when, at your physical location, you can wake up before and while the world itself is waking up. That is a beautiful and powerful time to meditate.

However, there is more deeply subtle knowledge to grasp here. The rising of the physical sun is symbolic of the obliteration of the dream and deep sleep states by the ignorant conscious waking state that is fully identified with the physical body.

The sun is also used as a symbol of the Self and the Heart on the right. However, here it represents the dawning of another day of ignorance. The moon, the queen of the night, symbolizes dreams and the luminosity of the purified mind.

The inner time in-between dreaming and waking is the Brahma Murta. It occurs every day for you even if you are a late sleeper. You can wake up at 11 in the morning and still access the true subjective Self-liberating "Brahma Murta."

The true Brahma Murta is the moment just when you are waking up but before you are fully identified with the physical body. In that moment, the Self displays itself. In that moment, you can directly awaken to the Self as your very own true Self.

STEP SIX: IS THE WAKING STATE IS BASED ON THE PHYSICAL BODY?

This ancient tradition of Brahma Murta gives us a clue about what the conscious waking state really is. By the way, if you find that is comes fairly easily to you to do meditation during the conventional Brahma Murta, meaning you awake in darkness and meditate as the day goes from early morning twilight into daylight, that's great. However, my opinion is that the personal display of the Self in the gap between sleep and waking is the more important Brahma Murta of the two.

I have never been an early riser. At one time, I did live with a community of yogis. We were all vegetarians who did hatha yoga. We would get up very early to meditate during the Brahma Murta hour. I was able to do it, but just barely.

I think since then probably the only time I have been awake at that hour is because I stayed up all night! I share this just to make the point that you don't have to get up real early to meditate. You can if you want to, and if you do, it may give you a slight advantage. When the world is quiet, the surrounding thought density is less.

Ultimately, follow your heart. Follow your deep inner guidance. Do whatever your inner guidance system is telling you to do. This is your intuition, the Self, talking.

What we are looking into right now is "What is the conscious waking state?"

Chances are you think you already know what it is. You are pretty sure it is this state where you are experiencing that you are the physical body. You are the doer as this physical body and you are walking around doing all of these things.

After all, you have to make a living. Plus you may have a relationship with somebody. Plus you have to feed the body, clothe the body, pay rent for a place to keep the body.

The list just goes on and on. This is the waking state of being the physical body in the physical world. You are fully identified with the body as yourself.

This is the typical experience of the conscious waking state. Having described it, I can tell you that it is a pile of junk, a pack of lies. If this is your experience of the conscious waking state, then you are hypnotized.

As you may know, when you hypnotize somebody, you use words to do so. You talk to them. Words, of course, are just thoughts. So you could say that what you are really using to hypnotize somebody is thoughts. Thoughts have the power to hypnotize people.

The most powerful single thought of all, by far, is the "I am the body" thought.

That may sound abstract, but the point is that what we are talking about here is your daily experience where you are feeling "I am this body named so and so and I do such and such in this very real big world that is outside of little physical me."

The typical waking state is a hypnotic state that has been reduced to a shadow of its former true Self due to the full adoption of this hypnotic command "You are your physical body." Once that command is accepted, then the person has the usual experience of daily life where they are living as and for the physical body.

However, what your conscious waking state REALLY IS is none other than the Self or pure Awareness. Let me repeat that. In answer to the question "What is my conscious waking state in reality?" the answer is... THE SELF... AWARENESS.

This is why it is said that you are "already enlightened" or you are "already the Self." Since you are participating in the conscious waking state, you have the "All Access Pass." You have full access, but you are not using it.

The very easiest time to make use of your Full Access Pass that was gifted to you because you were born as a human being is the subjective Brahma Murta time.

As I explained, when you come out of the dream state, you do NOT go directly into the physical body state. There is a gap, a break, a moment where the radiant Self or the Light of pure Awareness unveils itself and provides a full display and disclosure of its unbounded nature. This is a remarkable and incredible opportunity!

There is a GAP.

Notice this GAP.

Rest in this GAP.

You do not just go from deep sleep state to dream state to waking state. If that was true, then the only way you could have direct access to the Self would be if you could somehow stay conscious in the dark depths of unconsciousness that characterizes the usual deep sleep state (while you are sleeping at night).

The actual sequence of events is, keeping it simple, from deep sleep state to dream state to in-between state in which the spontaneous grace of the momentary full display of the Self takes place... and THEN typically there is the movement into the ownership claim for the physical body via the I-thought mental identification.

In sum, there is a GAP between deep sleep state and dream state. Then there is a GAP between dream state and waking state.

Deep sleep has a body. It is the causal body. Then...

> GAP.... *the Presence of Pure Radiant Consciousness.*

Dream state has a body. It is the dream body. Then...

> GAP.... *the Presence of Pure Radiant Consciousness.*

Waking state has a body. It is the physical body.

This is where you are now while reading about this GAP.

STEP SEVEN: WHAT IS THE CONSCIOUS WAKING STATE?

It is perhaps becoming obvious where I am going with this, but I will spell it out anyway. If you have figured it out, then congratulations are in order.

When the conscious waking state is not encumbered, controlled or hypnotized by the illusory delusional thought "I am the (physical) body," then the conscious waking state quite literally IS NONE OTHER THAN THE ENLIGHTENED SELF!

The conscious waking state in its original natural state IS pure self-luminous Awareness. It is the radiant Light of the Self. It is the spiritual Heart of Reality.

Perhaps this helps to illuminate how the spiritual teachers, Advaita or non-duality teachers especially, can be going around saying "You are the Self" and "You are already enlightened" and so on. How can that be?

Well, the way that that can be true in reality yet not true in your experience is that your conscious experience of yourself in your everyday normal waking state IS an experience of your true Self but it has been polluted and severely weakened.

So these statements could be reworded to say "In your conscious waking state, the treasure of the Self is already present. You have covered it over with your thoughts."

To be more specific, you have covered over your true Self with the false thief thought of "I am this physical body." That potent hypnosis is more than enough to steal from you your glorious birthright as the blessed supreme Self.

In the process of waking up from the sleeping state, there is a gap between dreaming and waking where the pure conscious state, the eternal non-state of the supreme Self, emerges and provides support for this major transition.

When you think about it, you are moving from one world to another. You are transitioning from the dream or astral universe to the the waking state or physical universe. This is a huge leap in vibrations and consciousness levels, so the Self itself emerges briefly in order to enable continuity during the transition.

Otherwise, the gap between the two levels would be so great as to produce a shock. But the main reason is that the mind becomes more aware of the truth of things when there is a sharp contrast between them. So if the sharp contrast between the dream or astral state and the physical body waking state was not buffered and smoothed out, then people would have this odd experience of literally jumping from the astral body into the physical body.

One of the consequences would be that everybody would then instantly know that they have at least two bodies, and the jig would be up. Although it is known that there is an astral body, this knowledge does not impact the physical body waking state except for the few who have been conscious during an astral body projection.

Being in the astral body while in the dream state, and then suddenly and without warning being conscious in the physical body waking state, it would be noticed that a major leap had occurred. In fact, the mechanism of being deluded into believing the hypnotic waking state is "real" is based upon the failure of memory.

If we remembered everything that happened during our sleeping, we would also realize that the physical body is playing just a minor role, not the major role we are hypnotized to believe in. If we remembered everything, then we would notice this gap. We would notice that the true Self arises as luminous Awareness and comes forward to fill in this gap and support this sudden transition.

However, unless you are looking for the Self in this gap, you are not likely to see it. This self-luminous Awareness is more subtle than dreams, although the practice of dream recall will support this practice of Self-recall in the morning. Anything that helps you insert the conscious waking state into the sleeping state may help.

Although this Awareness is extremely subtle, in this special moment it comes forward. Therefore, this is the time when it is most easily perceived and grasped.

The practice itself is very straightforward. If you cannot be aware of the entire waking up process itself, then immediately assert being consciously aware of your conscious awareness (waking state) the instant that you become aware of it.

In other words, the VERY INSTANT that you recognize that you have become conscious and are transitioning into the waking state associated with the physical body, in that instant you choose to WAKE UP. What happens is that you then wake up WITHIN THE GAP. You deliberately become conscious within this gap.

Even if this seems difficult at first, it really is the most natural thing for you to do. Waking up and automatically thinking and feeling that you are the physical body is just a habit. Like any other addiction, when you study it you start to discover spaces or gaps within the sequences that are typical of this addiction behavior.

You relax awake into clear seeing and an opening appears that you did not see before. This opening becomes your entry point from which you can unravel the entire addiction mechanism. Likewise, you can enter as lucid clear knowing when you wake up in the morning by using the special effortless Morning Meditation.

With practice, you will discover that you are not the body. In fact, you are the Light of the Awareness. The gap will get longer and longer. You will gain confidence that you are, indeed, the Self.

Eventually, you will be able to stabilize in the Self and your perception of who you are and what the world is will be changed forever. You will know directly from within that you are the Self and that the world is the Self. You will know for sure that "I AM THAT."

Yes, all of this is possible from studying, exploring and staying within this nearly invisible little gap between the sleeping state and the waking state. During that transitional window, the Self provides a full display for those who seek it.

Waking Up As Awareness

STEP EIGHT: WHO IS IT EXACTLY THAT CLAIMS THE BODY?

Now you know how to receive the darshan (full spiritual revelation and blessings) of your true Self when you wake up. We are almost ready to begin the methodical guidance in the precisely structured "Who am I?" or Self-inquiry meditation.

This two-step approach is a kind of "reverse engineering" that was developed by Sri Sadhu Om based upon his direct knowledge of how the I-thought arises. After learning it from him, I developed my version. I am sharing it with you here.

The plan is for you to do Self-awareness Morning Meditation in the "gap" when you wake up. With practice you discover for yourself how to extend the duration of this conscious Self-awareness and how to stay in it. The positive impact of doing this simple action in the morning is so great as to be beyond comprehension.

Even though it is something that takes place every morning, it is absolutely life-changing when it is engaged in consciously as you have been instructed. It will eventually dawn on you that the constant unbroken substrate of all of the states that are coming and going is this Self or pure Awareness that you met in the gap.

Even though it is true that the Self does come forward at the entry point into the waking state, this very same Self is present at all times in all places. It is always Here Now.

This is what you realize as you spend more and more time in the Self. It seems to expand, but then you see clearly that it did not "expand," it was already here and everywhere. The sacred darshan of radiant wide-open spaciousness in the morning is the proverbial "tip of the iceberg" of the true Self.

The foundation for the Self-inquiry meditation is to cultivate this understanding of the morning gap. Recognize that the Self as pure luminous Awareness is in fact arising as you emerge from the sleep state into the conscious waking state as the physical body. Incorporating this morning "stay in the gap" practice will overcome many of the obstacles that people have with the "Who am I?" type meditation.

If you are one of those people who believe in the astral body or dream body, consider what would happen if somehow you are flying around in your astral or dream body and then, for some strange reason, as you were all set to enter the physical body, this became impossible.

In this scenario, would you then wake up into and as the physical body?

The answer is that no, you would not. You would be stuck in the astral or dream realm.

This is not a hypothetical situation. Consider the scenario of someone who dies during their sleep. What happened to them?

The body died. Therefore, there is no physical vehicle for them to return to.

The person went to sleep in the normal way. Perhaps they accessed the deep sleep state and then had dreams. But on their way to return to the physical body, for health reasons or due to foul play, the physical flesh body was terminated.

The usual dilemma for the person who wants to do the "Who am I?" meditation is that they are already fully identified with the physical body at the time that they wish to do the meditation. Frankly, if you are fully identified with the physical body, then what answer do you expect other than "I am the physical body"?

At that moment, the mind is in complete belief that it is the body. So, in a way, that is the correct answer for that particular limited state.

However, going back to our theoretical scenario of the person who was dreaming and flying around in their astral body in the dream state before they tried to come back to the physical body, if that person could ask the question "Who am I?" what would their answer properly be?

Their answer would be "I am the body," but in this case it would be the ASTRAL or DREAM body, NOT the physical body. Isn't that interesting?

Now there are those who are very good at dream yoga or lucid dreaming who do this sort of inquiry or something similar in the dream state, which is wonderful. As far as I can tell, this sort of practice is beyond the reach of the average person.

The average person, though, will be going to sleep and waking up. So I have pointed to that morning transition point or gap in the familiar day to day 24 hour waking-deep sleep-dreaming-waking cycle. Dream yoga is not required.

Either way, what you are becoming conscious of is that which is able to make the observation and then the claim that "I am this particular body."

So whether you are claiming the physical body or the astral (dream) body as yourself, there is something that is able to do that and assert that claim.

Since this something that is obviously not asserting itself as a body or location is the one which is asserting that it is this or that body, the physical or the astral, then we have a most interesting conundrum.

How can it be that we are able to assert that we are this body?

We are asserting that we are this or that body, yet we are doing it from a place of not yet having a body.

In order to do this, we must first notice and observe this body. Then, having observed it, now we must identify it as our body in contrast to all of the other bodies around here. Finally, having observed it and positively identified it as the body that belongs to us, then we step in and claim it.

My goodness, that is an awful lot of stuff for "something" to be doing even before any kind of body has been claimed! What in the blazes could be doing this?

What exactly is it that is able to observe, identify and claim a body, physical or astral, yet does not itself have a body yet? What could that be?

You may be tempted to answer that "It is the Self or Awareness" that does these things, that claims the body, but this is not really correct. In some ultimate sense, it is true, but in the immediate day to day practical sense it is not true.

What claims the body is the mind. You probably do not realize this yet, but the sneaky little "I am the body" thought, even though you are very familiar with it on a day to day basis, is not a gross or obvious or surface thought at all.

In fact, the "I am the body" thought is the most subtle thought of them all!

It is the secret basis, the seed, for the birth and growth of the mind. Whether you realize it or not, the mind is just a bunch of thoughts. The first thought, the one that gets all of that nonsense going, is none other than the "I am the body" thought.

Here is what is going on. This "I am the body" thought can live for a short amount of time "between bodies." As you may know, you don't just have a physical body. You also have an astral (dream state) body and a casual (deep sleep state) body.

The mind per se can be associated with the physical, astral or causal body. The seed of the mind is this "I am the body" thought.

This "I am the body" thought must literally *hop* or *jump* from one body or state or dimension to another during the sleeping process. It is at its most vulnerable when it is jumping from one level of consciousness to another. It is naked and exposed.

These are its three stations or homes. In the course of the 24 hour day and night sleep and wake cycle, it keeps moving from "house (body) to house (body)."

There is a fourth station, the Self itself, but it is the underlying foundation Reality for all of the transitions between the stations. Because the Self or the Light of pure Awareness is the underlying foundation for ALL of the states, this means it is present during ALL of the transitions from one state or station to the other.

One way to think about the Self is that it is the deep sleep state or third station made conscious so that it is recognized during the waking state. Then the person knows that they are the Self, pure Awareness, and not the body or the mind.

So the special Morning Practice that I have been making such a big deal about is exactly such a transition or gap between stations in which the Self is present as the support. You may notice that the Self is also present in the transitions from the physical body to the astral body, from the astral body to the causal body and back again. Those doing dream yoga utilize these more subtle self-luminous transitions.

More precisely, these jumps from one body or station to the other are literal GAPS. Think of this gap as a BREAK.

If the Self or the Light of Awareness did not come forward at those times, the whole system would break down. Not only would the real nature of it all be exposed, it simply would not work. The total mechanism of life would collapse.

Here is the reason I have been talking about this more esoteric idea of subtle bodies. The "I am the body" thought is having to jump from one of these bodies to another of these bodies. Each time it jumps, it has to identify the body and claim it.

Keeping things simple, that means it is hopping like a frog from the physical body in the waking state to the astral body in the dream state to the causal body in the deep sleep state. In the deep sleep state it gets to rest and get regenerated.

The physical and astral bodies are regenerated by the deep sleep state, too, as it is the closest to the Self. Deep sleep is the Self when its ignorance is lifted.

As the I-thought hops from one body to another, all in relation to the same person, it exposes itself. It is naked, vulnerable and unprotected. It is able to make this leap from one station to another and expose itself only for brief periods of time.

This "I am the body" thought, the essence of the mind, is the one that is doing the identifying and claiming of your bodies. Physical, astral, causal, the I-thought doesn't care as long as it has a body to claim and use as its temporary home.

The reality is that the I-thought or I-am-the-body thought cannot last very long at all if it does not claim some sort of body or vehicle. So it is very vulnerable during the gap.

Most people have no clue about it or what it is doing every day and night, hopping from body to body, so it is in little danger from the vast majority of the human population. It takes a deep dedication to identify it and catch it doing its jumps.

In terms of the effortless special Morning Meditation Practice, what you are doing is being vividly present as an observer or witness of this very subtle "I am the body" thought as it jumps from the astral or dream body and the astral or dream station into the physical body and the waking state station. Since this jump and then reclaiming of the body does take a little bit of time, there is the opportunity to see this I-thought actually do this action where it falsely claims the body as itself.

So I'm not talking about aimlessly floating around in some vague "happy space" right after you wake up. I'm not talking about hanging out all groggy and blurry.

I am saying be sharply awake and aware like the touch of a knife blade. You are WAITING for the sneaky appearance of this I-thought and watching very closely in order to see how it operates with your own eyes and know the truth for yourself.

When you wake up first in the morning as the self-luminous Awareness, then you are ready for it. The "I am the body" thought comes bumbling in like some drunken fool only to discover that the light is on and his spouse is waiting for him!

He was expecting to do his usual selfish actions under cover of darkness and take over the "house" (the physical body). But now the lights are on and conscious Awareness is awake and aware to witness how he claims the body and steals it.

The "Who am I?" question has a specific direction and purpose. Its goal is to strike a crippling blow of doubt into this arrogant thought assertion "I am the body."

As your doubt of the thought "I am the body" increases, your ability to stay in the effortless Morning Meditation deepens. What matters most is the QUALITY and INTENSITY of your conscious and aware participation in that GAP.

Since typically the hypnotic idea "I am the body" has been taken as fact, you could say that the real question is "Am I really the physical body like I think I am?"

Put slightly differently, instead of "Who am I?" you could ask yourself "Am I really this body?" And also "If I am not the body, then who or what am I?"

Another reason I mentioned the astral or dream body here is to make it clear that just because you have a subtle body of some kind, your situation has not changed very much. Your subtle body will have different powers, but you are still stuck in a body. There is still domination by the master control thought "I am the body."

To think and be convinced that you are the physical body is living in an iron prison. To believe that you are the life force (chi or prana) body that co-exists with the physical is living in a bronze prison. To believe that you are the creative astral body is living in a silver prison. To believe that you are the blissful causal body is living in a golden prison. They are all prisons, whatever the bars may be made of.

Waking Up As Awareness

STEP NINE: THE PRACTICAL TWO-STEP "WHO AM I?" MEDITATION

Now that we have laid the groundwork for the spontaneous realization of the Self and spiritual enlightenment, I can talk about the "Who am I?" or Self-inquiry meditation proper.

Now you understand why this two-step format for the question came about and why it is so effective and powerful.

The big question of life, the only real crisis that any of us have, is the identity question. When you answer that question to your satisfaction, as long as you came up with something that seems to work for you, you can proceed with your life with renewed strength and sense of direction.

Once you have solved the identity question according to your needs and standards, then the rest of life is just details. The biggest question, the biggest problem that we struggle with and must answer from within as human beings is "Who am I?"

If you read everything up to here, then you know that the question "Who am I?" can have more than one answer. The answer that you give depends on the experience that you are having right now. For example, if you are having the experience that you are the physical body, then that is the answer you will give.

If you are lucid in the dream state, then you might answer the question by saying "I am this dream body."

Yet when you return to the everyday waking state, your answer to the same question is now "I am this physical body."

Of course, you are the Self, but this will be your reply if you answer directly from your hypnosis.

Since we have identified that there are three states or stations, and each has a body to go with it, then we can confidently observe that there are only three, or perhaps, seven conventional answers to the great question of "Who am I?" As we will see, the number seven applies if the pathways between the stations get included.

There are three answers and the three stations if we do not include the Self or the ever present Light of pure Awareness as a station. Some people do.

People do not typically assert "I am the blissful peaceful causal body," but they will say that they remember being in a deep dreamless restful state. They may say, based on their recall of their experience the night before, "I was the causal body."

If you include the Self, then the four stations are that you are the physical body, the astral body, the casual body or you are the Self. Being all-present, the Self is not a station per se, but we are including it here to put forth a simple model.

Since the Self neither comes nor goes, but is simultaneously and universally present in all the states as itself as well as its own station, we prefer to talk here just about three stations: the physical station, the astral station, the causal station.

The other four answers, to add up to seven, would be the response you might make if you were answering from within one of the transition states. For example, while you are doing the effortless special Morning Meditation inside of the "gap," you are working within the transitional space that is between the astral or dream state body and the physical or waking state body. Your honest answer in that moment to "Who am I?" would be "At present, I am the gap BETWEEN dream and waking."

These four transition states are waking to dream, dream to causal, causal back to dream, dream back to waking. I am describing it as four because the experience, for example, of going from waking to dream is is different from going from dream to waking from the perspective of those bodies. Likewise, moving from the causal body to the dream body is different than going from dream body to causal body.

Ultimately, there is no difference, but the subjective experience is not the same.

(Note: My observations are in accord with the famous *Mandukya Upanishad*. I'm just emphasizing the gaps between the stations of consciousness more than it does).

Although in the scientific model we go first to deep sleep and not directly to dreaming (REM sleep), in order to do so we pass through levels of consciousness that correspond to the dream realm. We just don't dwell in them at that stage. The body knows that deep sleep is the most important state.

As we have emphasized, the Self or the Light of pure Awareness comes forward in EACH of transitional state.

In summary, we have three stations and four transitional states. The so-called "Fourth" station is the Self, which is omnipresent in all of the stations and in all of the change or transition states (gaps or jumps). If we include the Self, then we have four and four or eight possible responses.

The transitions between the three "body stations" take place very quickly, so you must be on your toes to catch what is happening within them and see the Self or supreme Light. It can be done. It begins by gaining the knowledge here.

If you are deeply engaged in an in-between state at that time, then your honest answer might be "I am neither physical, astral nor causal. I am currently identified with an in-between transition state." But as you know, you can go deeper still.

If you are able to go even deeper with that observation, which is what happens as do the special Morning Meditation practice (after all, you already are the Self), then that observation blossoms into "I am neither physical, astral nor causal. I am currently identified with THE LIGHT OF SELF AWARENESS that is ALWAYS present in this transition state from the astral body going to the physical body."

As the ability to dwell in the unbounded Light of Awareness is cultivated and expanded, then it will begin to permeate your waking state life. You will begin to enjoy a lightness of being, the peace and joy and feeling of freedom that is possible only for those who are setting themselves free from the limited mind.

That you have positively identified the Light of the Self at the secret juncture of the waking state is the foundation for the blossoming of your true Self-realization. Your insight grows to see that this Self or Awareness, which is always present in the morning transition state, is always present in ALL situations and states.

In what will probably be an effortless process, you will simply begin to see that everything around you (1) quite literally IS you and (2) quite literally IS the SELF.

Obviously, then, you are the Self. The World is the Self and the Self is All. Everything IS the SELF. There is only the Self. I am the Self. I AM THAT.

If you don't care for the language of "astral body," then just substitute "dream body" or "dream state." The language is unimportant. What is important is that you understand in your own way what the instructions are for the Morning Exercise.

Assuming that you did your Morning Meditation, or even if you did not, here is the formal Self-inquiry meditation or "Who am I?" meditation that I teach.

TWO-STEP "WHO AM I?" (SELF-INQUIRY) MEDITATION

(1) WHEN A THOUGHT ARISES, CHALLENGE IT.

(2) YOU CHALLENGE IT BY ASKING "WHO IS HAVING THIS THOUGHT?"

(3) THIS THOUGHT WILL ANSWER "I AM."

(4) YOU THEN CHALLENGE THAT THOUGHT AND ASK "WHERE DID YOU COME FROM?"

(5) THIS THOUGHT WILLTHEN BE SILENCED. IT IS REALLY JUST THE I-THOUGHT OR THE I-AM-THE-BODY THOUGHT PRETENDING TO BE THE OWNER OF THE BODY. SINCE YOU HAVE NOW "BUSTED" THIS I-THOUGHT AND EXPOSED IT, IT RETREATS BACK INTO ITS SOURCE.

NOTE: ANY KIND OF "INQUIRY" CAN WORK. THIS IS NOT THE ONLY STYLE THAT IS EFFECTIVE. A MODERN STYLE OF INQUIRY IS BEING TAUGHT BY BYRON KATIE.

THE MAIN THING IS TO CHALLENGE EACH THOUGHT. DO NOT ACCEPT YOUR THOUGHTS AT FACE VALUE. DO NOT BELIEVE YOUR THOUGHTS. YOUR MIND IS JUST MAKING STUFF UP. YOUR MIND IS JUST A MACHINE THAT MAKES STUFF UP. IT IS A DREAM MACHINE. IT IS YOUR PERSONAL "HOLLYWOOD." IT IS ALL MADE UP.

In a paradox that is not easy to understand at first, this real "source" for the I-thought, the place or home that this false "I am the body" thought runs back to is none other than the Self or the Heart! It is beyond the scope of this 12 step guide to explain this apparent contradiction, but when find that you are discovering that the Self or Heart or Awareness is the real source, you are on the right track!

You could also say that the secret "hideout" for this master thief "I am the body" thought is the dark mysterious deep sleep cave of the causal body. That is why investigations at the physical body or dream body levels do not catch it. The I-thought renews itself in the causal body, then sneaks out to dominate other bodies.

The step by step meditation described above is the exact meditation that I have used with excellent results. It is because this specific form of the "Who am I?" meditation has helped me so much, I am sharing it with you now. It seems that after studying every Self-inquiry technique under the sun, I found this one.

Please feel free to adapt the words to your own needs. But I strongly recommend that you keep it just as it is in the structure, as a two-step question format.

Although it appears to have many steps, really there are just two steps. These are the two questions. You ask two questions, not one. If you were to just ask "Who am I?" then you would just get the I-thought masquerading as the true "I."

You can ask "Who am I?" over and over so that you challenge the first I-thought.

Or you can keep asking over and over "Who is this I?" Through repetition, you might wear down the I-thought so that it shuts up and sits still for awhile.

Some people find that repeating "I-I" over and over again like a mantra is highly effective. This keeps the mind centered on just the I-thought and the pure I-feeling. In the resulting thought-free state, they dive deep into the Silence, into the Heart.

This advice to repeat "I-I" is direct from Sri Ramana Maharshi. It is reliable. If you like to do mantras as a meditation, then this form of Self-inquiry may be ideal for you.

I have personally found, after trying out many variations over a period of years, that the above two-step question format is the most simple, elegant and direct Self-inquiry method possible. It is "reverse engineered" from how the I-thought operates daily.

The reason it is so effective is that it is based on what the I-thought actually does with the body to take it over. It rises up to the head from the Heart (causal body).

Then it spreads from the top of the head down all over the body like a sticky deadening goo. This creates the pervasive persuasive "I am the body" feeling.

It is like the I-thought uses a secret nerve drug to dope people up and make them feel they are the body. It is like a nerve toxin that creates a deceptive solidity and density to the flesh.

If the I-thought stayed stuck in the head as just a casual floating thought, the hypnosis would not be convincing. Because people FEEL it, they tend to BELIEVE it. Even so, it is all just a very clever hypnosis act by the I-thought!

It is this feeling that pervades the entire physical body that is so convincing. Since the average person investigating the nature of the "I" and doing the "Who am I?" question is starting from a state of body feeling that is completely drenched in the waking state "I am the body" experience, they have two strikes against them.

However, there is more to it than that. For one thing, you have to catch the thought right when it arises. The other thing is that you want to be paying attention to where the I-thought goes when it falls away. Where or what is its "source"?

You must identify it for yourself. Just hearing about it isn't enough.

For some meditators, the awareness develops that the I-thought arises from the causal Heart on the right. It shoots up from the Heart on the right up to the head.

When you challenge it in the two-step question and it retreats back to where it came from, that source will be discovered to be the Heart on the right side of the chest. While the ability to see this is useful, I know that it is not required.

Not everybody sees, senses or feels the Heart on the right. The main thing is to persistently challenge the I-thought. As you do this, you will experience longer and longer breaks without thoughts. This will bring you a welcome inner peace.

Remember, the first time you ask "Who am I?" or "Who are you?", the answer is coming from the I-thought since it has already claimed the body in the morning.

That is why you ask "Where do you come from?" or "What is your source?" next right away. The one-two punch is needed to knock out the I-thought!

The real Self or true Awareness has no "voice." It is ultimate Silence itself. It is without thoughts. Therefore, you know you are in the Self when you are resting in the thought-free spaciousness. If thoughts are coming up and replying to your questions, you are not talking to the Self! You are talking to the I-thought!

In deep Self-inquiry meditation, the verbalization of the questions falls away. It is replaced by pure silent feeling and dwelling in the joy and peace of the Heart. So if the technique falls away, that's okay as long as you are resting in spacious Silence. This is the natural state of effortless freedom.

The investigation continues as a deep feeling-sensing. The rising thoughts are actually quite substantial and gross in the material sense compared to the Heart. Intuitive investigation with heart-felt feeling-sensing will make this become clear. The true nature of thought as crude matter substance shows that is just a trap or prison for the pure Awareness. Seeing that clearly, you want nothing to do with it. You want the Heart.

STEP TEN: HOW TO DO "WHO AM I?" MEDITATION DURING THE DAY

What I just described is the convenient sitting practice.

Catching thoughts and challenging them so that they return to their source (the Heart) may not be easy at first. If you find it challenging while sitting quietly in meditation at home or on a retreat, you will discover that it is even more difficult while you are busy doing things in the world.

That said, when I was in this phase of my meditation practice, I found that there were many windows of opportunity during the course of the day. For example, if you take a bus or train to work, as I was at the time, you have an opportunity to sit quietly, catch your thoughts as they arise, and challenge them with the two steps.

In fact, meditating in the world is easier than most people think. From my participation over the years in numerous meditation and self-help "cultures," I can say that many people have three things wrong about meditation.

The first error is that they think you must do meditation sitting down under ideal quiet circumstances. The second error is thinking that meditation has to be for a long time, for at least 20 minutes or more. The third error is thinking that the longer the meditation session, the better.

Quality, not quantity, is the key. Be focused and concentrated while you are doing Self-inquiry, even if it's just five minutes.

Two to five minutes of concentrated Self-inquiry can be highly effective when you are on the go. This is especially true as your meditation progresses. It is a skill you can develop.

Like a ninja master, you become more adept at jumping in with your sword of inquiry and slicing up the distracting thoughts. Even if you have to go back to work or something else that keeps your mind busy, you will feel a residual peace from the few short minutes of two-step "Who am I?" meditation that you did.

Maybe we can call it "guerrilla meditation" or "stealth meditation," but this is a very good approach. If you have to spend most of your week working and then just have the weekend or the equivalent off from work, think in terms of "stealing" a few minutes of meditation here or there. Thoughts drop. Your peace grows.

If you are given only half an hour or so for lunch at work, take just five minutes and sit quietly where you will not be bothered. Knowing that you have only a handful of minutes, do the two-step "Who am I?" meditation with great intensity.

Due to your sense of urgency, this may work out very well. We can become complacent when we follow the same comfortable meditation routine every day.

We may also fall into the trap of thinking that "meditation" is only when we are "sitting." Meditation, ultimately, is realizing the Self that is always present.

Notice that the "Who am I?" question is not for the Self. The Self or Awareness already knows who or what it is!

The question is for the body-identified self, the I-thought. It is the body-based sense of self that is asking this question "Who am I?" The reason it is asking this question is that the identity has found itself in a strange place, in an experience that is alien to its unbounded nature. It has found itself to be stuck in a body.

Ironically, it is the I-thought that is asking this question. The I-thought or "I am the body" thought is the very essence of ignorance. It is ignorance itself. So even though it is behind the mechanism that creates the forgetting of the Self as the true self, it also manages to forget that it is itself the culprit behind all this madness.

The I-thought is very confused. It feels compelled to do whatever it needs to do in order to survive, but it does not have a sophisticated understanding of what it is doing. Even so, it is the most formidable opponent you will ever encounter.

The I-thought is like a thief who breaks into your house and steals your most valuable possessions. Yet when confronted by the police, he has a most convenient case of amnesia. Even when he is captured in the Heart, as long as he stays functional he is a threat. Like a career criminal, he never wants to give up his agenda. His survival is all he knows and he desires it at any cost.

Q&A: SELF-INQUIRY MEDITATION WHEN DOING ACTIVITIES

Q: Do I need to challenge every thought?

A: Ramana Maharshi says you should. While doing sitting meditation where you can give your full attention to the inquiry, then the answer is yes, to the best of your ability.

While you are busy during the day, you want to at least cultivate being aware of the arising of thoughts even if you are not in a position at that moment to challenge and dismantle each thought as it rises up.

This is a matter of self-education. You want to see for yourself the impact of your thoughts. It is your thoughts that produce your suffering, not your circumstances per se. You also want to eventually see and know for yourself that of all the many thoughts that come and go, they all depend on the master hypnotist thought "I am the body." This thought is the ring leader of the thoughts that gang up on you.

When you are at home or on a retreat, or on public transport to and from work, or taking a five minute break during lunch to meditate, then your goal is to be aware of each thought AS IT ARISES and challenge it AS SOON AS POSSIBLE. Don't let it gain any momentum. Confront it with the two-step as soon as you notice it. Be aggressive. Knock it down. Really, you want to knock it out!

Q: But what if I have trouble even noticing my thoughts rising? What can I do?

A: Ramana said it was okay to repeat "I-I" or "I am." You can do this as a mantra to keep yourself centered, but do it with the understanding that the meaning of this "mantra" is that you are working at remembering your true "I," your real Self.

If you were to say to me "I" or "I-I," my response would be "Very good, very good!" That is what you are -- I or I am. But when you add to it the qualifiers that are based on identifying with the physical body, so that then you say "I am so and so and I do such and such," that it is not true. That is your hypnosis.

You can express it like this as a formula.

Your Real "I" = YOUR First Person "I" FEELING Now

MINUS

The false "I am the body" thought.

This first person feeling of being "I" that you have RIGHT NOW is the feeling of your real Self, only it is being limited and bounded by the body-based I-thought.

Without the I-thought confining you, you are unbounded pure Being-Feeling. This is why it is said "You are already That." The reason is that your First Person Feeling of existing is right, but the sense that you are limited is wrong. You are the unlimited "I." Any sense of limitation or bondage is from the "I am the body" idea.

To be and rest in this pure unbounded Being-Feeling without any thought conditioning IS to be totally happy, at peace, filled with joy, overflowing with love and so on. These expansive highly desirable positive feeling states that all people yearn for is the very nature of who you are when the I-thought is not interfering.

You ARE Happiness. You ARE Peace. You ARE Love.

You ARE Joy. You ARE Freedom. You ARE Universal Pure BEING.

Being is not an abstract at all. Being is the natural FEELING of Being that you are already familiar with. Your ability to experience it has been weakened by thought.

If your identity feels small, insignificant, it is handcuffed by the tyrant I-thought. Your True Identity is not little or subservient. Once it throws off the harsh shackles of the I-thought, this Feeling of Being is the ONE INFINITE "I"!

So if you cannot challenge the thoughts, repeat "I-I-I" like that. Or do a more conventional mantra that refers to the Self, such as "Om Namah Shivaya" or "Jai Kali Ma." The mantra helps to keep you centered until you have an opportunity where you can return to noticing, capturing and conquering each thought.

Q: Are we always just fighting thoughts like this? Does it ever end?

A: It may sound like you're fighting with thoughts or that it's hard work, but it is not like that. These rising thoughts are like thieves that up until now have been boldly breaking into your house and stealing you blind, robbing you of your most precious possessions -- your happiness, your peace, your love and so on.

Now that you are catching these thieves and kicking them out of your house, what could be more joyful than that? How wonderful! At long last, I have found the key to getting rid of those rascals! At last I can have my peace and joy! Oh, happy day!

As you progress, you spend more and more time resting in the Self. This means you rest in a beautiful naturally thought-free space. It feels like you have come home and now you just rest in your natural state of Being. There is nothing else like it. It is what everybody is pursuing with their drugs and luxury items and all of that, trying to feel good. When you get rid of the thoughts, you are there.

As your sensitivity to the limiting nature of thoughts grows, you will not tolerate these arrogant thoughts stealing your happiness. You will defend your Being. The average person is unaware that the happiness these thoughts are allowing them is but a dribble. They stand next to a big rushing river of joy yet their thoughts allow them a tiny cup now and then.

When you see how your thoughts are ripping you off, you get very motivated. Once you have tasted the peace and joy of your natural state, then you want to have it more and more. You realize that it is your birthright.

The peace, joy, love and so on is already in your possession since it is your nature. The thoughts cover it up and then make you think the problem, the cause, is outside of you. In fact, the thoughts themselves are the problem!

Let your thoughts go and all your problems will go with them. The experience of having a "problem" that you need to solve is itself a product of thoughts.

Life becomes simple. There will still be challenges, but your experience will be that they are handled automatically by life.

STEP ELEVEN: PEACE NOW FROM THE "WHO AM I?" MEDITATION

Eventually, as you persist with the three meditation times, the gap in which the Light can be seen, sensed, felt, perceived or otherwise known expands, widens and deepens. The access gets easier and the length of time in which you have conscious access gets longer.

Each time you drop a thought with the two-step "Who am I?" meditation, you are reducing your stress and increasing your peace. The burden of psychological pressure that people feel is the build up of these accumulated thoughts.

As you release and dissolve thoughts with this meditation, your "thought load" gets lighter. In the Self or Awareness, there are no thoughts. There is only deep Joy and beautiful Peace. Life goes on but you don't have to carry a heavy "bag of thoughts" every day. There are still challenges, but life becomes very simple.

The deeply restful Peace of the deep sleep state begins to permeate your waking state. This affects everything in your whole life. As this elegant process unfolds, you will find that your life itself becomes a source of profound revelation for you.

You can expect that life itself will get easier for you and more enjoyable. The way of Self-inquiry meditation or "Who am I?" meditation is compatible with everyday life.

This includes being married and raising a family. Stress is reduced. Health is improved. The feeling of happiness and deep restful peace more and more becomes the baseline of your experience.

More than any other meditation approach that I am familiar with, this method of realizing the Self and encouraging the Dawning of Awareness is gentle, easy going and based, even from the beginning, on peace and joy. As the peace and joy grow, then the fruits of love also reveal themselves. It is a beautiful path!

The three meditation times are, of course, the effortless special Morning Meditation, 20 minutes of sitting meditation a day (at least) and any "stealth" meditation minutes you were able to grab while out in the world. You should notice the benefits in terms of reduced worry and less stress right away.

If you are really gung ho or you have an affinity for sleep and dream yoga, then you can add a fourth meditation time and meditate while falling asleep. If you can do Self-inquiry in dream yoga, then by all means go ahead.

Any of the four transitions -- waking to dream, dream to causal, causal to dream, dream to waking -- can be accessed as a silent luminous spiritual gap. Then the inquiry into the true nature of the Self as the always present supporting Light of Awareness is engaged.

Q&A: THE PEACE THAT RESULTS FROM THIS MEDITATION

Q: I think everybody would like less stress. What is this peace you talk of?

A: My best answer would be "Do the 'Who am I?' meditation and see for yourself."

If you or somebody else asking this question is heavily dominated by their thoughts, which really means by the I-thought or "I am the body" thought, then their idea of getting relaxed and feeling some peace is to have a couple of stiff drinks or smoke a marijuana joint!

Well, for that person, relatively speaking, that is their peace. That is how they get free from stress. Even if it does make them feel a little better for a little while, they have done nothing about their thought stress burden that they carry every day.

The real key is to do the two-step meditation until the light comes on where you see just how profoundly and negatively you are being impacted by your rising thoughts. Until that day comes, you will think that you can take it or leave it.

Your circumstances in life may be pretty good, your thoughts may seem fairly positive, so you don't feel motivated to do the Self-inquiry. If you are enjoying such a time in your life, then this is the time you will want to make an extra effort. Your karma is positive and you have the free time. After all, if you meditate an hour a day, everything in your life will go better.

You must see for yourself the real nature of thoughts and how they are limiting your happiness and your freedom and your peace, limiting you from the moment you wake up, actually torturing you and adding to your life an absolutely massive burden of suffering. All of your thoughts are limiting you!

The peace I talk of is your true nature. It is your natural state.

To be limited and confined by your thoughts is unnatural. You have been hypnotized into believing that a new job or new car or new drug or new lover will make you happy.

What really happens is that for a moment, due to the freshness and unfamiliarity of that new experience, your thought burden gets a little lighter. The mind briefly stops. The cloud cover of the mind parts briefly. The Sun of the Self, of the pure thought-free state, shines through in its glorious radiance.

In that short period of time, in the gap between thoughts, the joy of the Self shines through. Then the thought clouds return, dark and heavy, and block out the Sun of the Self again.

Q: Does there come a time when I don't have to do the two-step Self-inquiry? It seems to me that since I'm using thoughts, they would have to go at some point?

A: The two-step inquiry meditation does consist of thoughts, or you could say a verbalization. But it is not intellectual and it is not really coming from your head.

Even the I-thought, with all its arrogance and boldness, is not foolish enough to play the role of destroying itself.

The special thoughts of the two-step meditation are carefully designed to challenge the rising I-thought and send it back to its source with its tail between its legs. What that means is that these thoughts are really coming from the Self! Their origin is Silence, the Heart.

Because in the past I had done meditation techniques where you just sit and passively watch thoughts, I had the idea that my goal was to arrive at a state where I had no thoughts. So when I would have a good day of meditation with not too many thoughts, I was reluctant to go back to using the two-step verbalization.

But then it dawned on me one day that I was wrong. My silence, a quiet state of the mind to which I was strongly attached, was really more of a pseudo-silence.

When you just watch thoughts without striking them down, things do quiet down a bit, but the reality is that the thoughts are just hiding out. Like thieves waiting for you to go to bed so they can rob you, they are lurking just below the surface.

So my mental quiet was not really true "peace" at all. It was a trance state or some other quieted state, but since the thoughts were allowed to exist just under the surface, I did not feel deeply peaceful and content and happy. I felt more of a blank, almost a numbness. This bothered me and I couldn't figure it out. According to the teaching of just watching thoughts, I should be feeling a full positive joyful deeply restful peace.

So I challenged my apparently "quiet" state and returned to the two-step meditation and took on the thoughts as they rose up. After some time, I found that the deep quiet had returned, only this time there was a qualitative difference. I felt truly happy, deeply peaceful, genuinely joyful. It was rich and fulfilling. Finally, I was free of the "mental blank" state.

I knew right away it was because I had been challenging the thoughts and knocking them down. Now they were not lurking just beneath the surface. I did not have thought thieves circling my house at night. This was truly blissful rest!

When you have realized the Self, thoughts will come and go but none of it will matter. Thoughts need to arise at times to help the body perform tasks. The Silence remains and is untouched because the Self itself is without thoughts or thinking.

Even the two-step meditation may arise. Whatever thought is needed shows up.

The meditator thinks they are doing this two-step meditation as a technique. In fact, the spiritual super-power of Self-attention is doing the work. The words act as a focal point for the force of awareness. They are a sword in the hands of truth.

Or they are the paint and paint brush for a great artist. This artist is the Self. When the words fall away, what is left is the Self-attention. It was there all along, but the fog of thoughts hid it. Like a beautiful tropical island of peace, it was there, but in the confusion, it could not be seen. Eventually, when the Sun comes out and stays out, everything is answered. All that is left is to live in this paradise.

Thoughts themselves have a practical value. They are not a problem as long as the body-based I-thought, the "I am the body" idea, is not in command. When the I-thought takes over and is running the show -- the usual experience -- the Heaven on Earth that is Being the Self is transformed into a literal "hell on earth."

Q: What about the Heart on the right? Are we supposed to experience that?

A: Some people do, some people don't. It is not a prerequisite for Self-realization or enlightenment. Ramana experienced it so he talked about it. He is not the only one. Many of his disciples who attained enlightenment did.

Papaji, the guru of the well-known American teacher Gangaji, experienced it in Ramana's presence. There is no question of Gangaji's enlightenment, yet as far as I know, she did not experience the Heart on the right nor does she talk about it.

I have experienced it often. In fact, I would have to say it has played a major role in my spiritual practice. However, Ramana is very clear that this seeing, feeling, sensing or intuiting of the Heart on the right is not needed. It is just a reference point relative to the physical body for the causal body or deep sleep center.

I believe that if you do experience it, it will act as an inspiration. I know that seeing its warm glow, like a happy little golden sun at the right side of my chest, has been a major motivator for me.

But the Heart on the right was rarely talked about before Ramana showed up, so we can be sure that it is not needed.

Q: If you do sense the Heart on the right, or even if you don't, how is this related to thoughts? You said earlier that it is the source of thoughts?

The Heart on the right is the signature of the Self in the physical body. The Self or the pure Being-Feeling "I" is none other than your first-person "I" set free of the limitations imposed by the "I am the body" thought hypnosis. The Self or pure true unconditioned Being-Feeling "I" is without thoughts or limitation. The Self is completely thought-free. It has no thoughts and it has never had any thoughts.

However, in what is a paradox, at the practical day to day level, you will see that the I-thought, the "I am the body" thought, rises up out of the Heart on the right to the head. It is only once the I-thought rises up and then sits down in the head, gets comfortable there, so to speak, that he can go to work and cause so much trouble.

So the trouble making thoughts are hiding out latent in the Heart. Then they rise up to the head where they become active. It begins in the morning when you wake up.

There is the window where the Heart or Self comes forward and there is a no-thought state. Then the "I am the body" thought leaps up to the head and takes over, spreading its hypnotic illusion throughout the nerves and all through the body. This is what convinces people that they literally are the physical body.

As you do the meditation, sooner or later you will naturally begin resting in Silence, which is resting in the Heart or Self. At that time, perhaps before, you may have the experience of being drawn to the Heart on the right. You may feel it pulling you there, like a friendly magnet.

To me this makes sense. The causal body is waking up. It is going from darkness to Light. Plus what could possibly be more magnetic and attractive than the Heart?

The Heart on the right beginning to glow is a strong sign of this awakening. However, it is just a sign. It is not found in all traditions and it is not necessary. A sign is a sign, not the awakening.

Q: Why are there two steps? Why not just one step of asking "Who am I?"

A: The way that thoughts take over the body actually has two steps, and this is why this kind of Self-inquiry or "Who am I?" meditation also has two steps. We are reversing the sequence of events. It is very logical once you understand it.

In the morning, the "I am the body" thought rose up to the head and took over the body. Then it began issuing hypnotic commands as the phony dictator. So the two steps in the morning are (1) the I-thought rises up to the head and (2) the I-thought starts giving orders as if it is the boss. The deluded person becomes its puppet.

The two-step Self-inquiry "Who am I?" meditation effectively reverses this process. So first you ask something like "Who is having this thought?"

The reason you ask the question that way is to get the answer from the I-thought. So the I-thought answers something like "I am." Remember, YOU are not having the thought and YOU could not possibly be having the thought. YOU are the Self.

So to conclude the first step, the I-thought answers and says it is having this thought. It is the owner of this thought. But we are not done yet. We know that no matter what the thought is about, behind it there is the master thought.

So in the second step, you ask something like "Where did you come from?" or "What did you come from?" or "Who are you?" or "Who is this I?" or "Who am I?" and THIS I-thought that claims the ownership falls back down into its source.

This I-thought that can claim the ownership of other thoughts is the "I am the body" thought. It is the King of Thoughts. All the other thoughts are its servants.

But when it is directly challenged, it will fall back. Why? Because it is the Self-attention that is challenging it, not just more words or thoughts.

The supreme Self itself, the pure Light of Awareness, is calling its bluff and saying "I-thought, you are a phony and you know it!"

Well, the con artist I-thought does know it. Ashamed of itself, it falls down.

So in that second step we precisely and directly reverse the rising up and claiming of the body that the "I am the body" thought did when you woke up in the morning. But it is not easily undone, so you have to undo it again and again.

As you keep undoing this possession of the body by the I-thought, you feel more open and free. Your experience of "I" expands. Your natural thought-free Identity starts asserting itself now that the shackles of the I-thought are being removed.

The first question makes the I-thought come forward and claim the current thought. This corresponds to the spreading of the I-thought from the head to cover the body so that it can falsely claim it as its personal property and possession.

The second question makes the I-thought admit that its original claim over the body is false. This corresponds to the first moment of waking up where the I-thought jumps up and claims the body before the Self can come forward.

Asking the second question in the form of what or where did you come from does not mean you are looking for it to fall back down into the Heart on the right. If you see that happen, fine. But the "where" is the Self itself, the pure Being, the Silence.

So when you challenge it in the second step with the second question, it will fall away. Then the point is to rest in the Silence and give you full attention to your Being. This is called Self-attention. To be still and rest in the Self is the ultimate inquiry, but most people need to do the daily work of thought challenging first.

Obviously, the more you can rest in this Stillness of Being, in the Self, the more you will be experiencing yourself AS the Self. So there comes a day when you realize that this first person "I" feeling that you have been experiencing all of your life that felt like you really is you.

YOU minus the limiting "I am the body" hypnosis ARE THE SELF!

So this feeling of "you" was right all along. The sense of limitation was false.

You and the unbounded always happy peaceful true Self are one and the same! This discovery is the most wonderful day of your life!

When a prisoner is convinced that he cannot escape, or even that he is not in a prison, then he will not bother to examine his shackles. But then a free person walks through the prison shouting "Look at your shackles! Look at your shackles! They are not locked. Stand up and walk. Your shackles will just fall off!"

When you stand up and start to walk out, the shackles just fall off. Suddenly, you are free. All you had to do was challenge the fake shackles of the I-thought. You realize you are free and you have always been free. You were the true "I" all along, but you had bought into the phony hypnosis from the master manipulator, the I-thought or "I am the body" thought. You are who you always were and always will be, the unbounded pure feeling of the happy peaceful free true "I."

STEP TWELVE: REVIEW, SUMMARY AND "WHAT COMES NEXT?"

As promised, I am now going to ask you the same questions that I asked you at the beginning of this "Who am I?" Self-inquiry meditation course.

Hopefully, you wrote your earlier answers down. If not, then please take a moment to reflect on what your understanding was before you started this course.

Okay, here are all 12 of the original questions from the first three Steps.

Please write your answers down in your journal or on a piece of paper or type them into your computer. Be sure to include a date.

I am not going to provide the "right" answers to these questions.

The "right" answer is to realize the Self. That brings an end to all questions.

Also, these and the other inquiry-type questions I provided here may or may not be the best questions for you. They were very useful for me, though.

Feel free to come up with your own questions. If you like, you can modify the practical two-step "Who am I?" meditation now that you understand how it works.

The reason that some people find that the "Who am I?" meditation doesn't seem to work for them is that if you just sit and ask "Who am I?", the Self is not going to answer. The only part of your waking state experience that is going to answer a thought in the form of a question... is another thought... the I-thought!

Since the Self is silent, asking a verbalized question within needs to be structured properly in order to turn the outgoing thought around and redirect it inwards. That is precisely what this wonderful two-step "Who am I?" meditation technique does.

I strongly suggest keeping the two steps, but you may find that you resonate more with other variations of the questions. Please feel free to experiment.

Just remember that the one who is answering the question is in fact the I-thought. You are directly challenging it so that it will go away -- ultimately, forever!

There is a good reason why it collapses and goes away when it is successfully challenged. It is a phony. Since this method gets to the root of the rising thoughts, the silence that results from this meditation is deep and true, from the Heart itself.

THE 12 QUESTIONS AGAIN

(1) What is the mind?

(2) What is the I-thought?

(3) What is the "I am the body" idea?

(4) What prevents you from being fully enlightened or Self-realized?

(5) Where is the mind?

(6) Where is the I-thought?

(7) Where is the "I am the body" idea?

(8) In relationship to your physical body, what is the location or identity or nature of what prevents you from being fully enlightened or Self-realized?

(9) Why do YOU want to do "Who am I?" or Self-inquiry meditation?

(10) Why or how does this question "Who am I?" naturally arise in the first place?

(11) Why is it that the mind asks this question but Awareness does not?

(12) Who exactly is asking this ultimate Big Question "Who am I?"

After asking or answering each question, feel free to go into meditation. Or you can meditate while you answer the questions. You can go into meditation to answer the question, then come back out to write it down.

Waking Up As Awareness

SUMMARY OF WHAT WE COVERED

(1) You as the conscious waking state are the unbounded totally free true Self (the Heart or Light of pure Awareness). You experience your "I" as pure feeling Being.

Your limited first person "I" feeling is the caterpillar for the true Self butterfly that feels completely free and unlimited. It has no thoughts. It only knows happiness.

(2) You don't have to go anywhere or do anything to be That. You Are It.

(3) Each morning as you transition from the sleep (dream) state to the conscious waking state, you go through a GAP. While you are in this GAP or transitional state BETWEEN the sleep/dream station and the waking state station, the Light of the Self comes forward in all of its glory.

(4) If you keep your body still without moving and maintain full alertness, you can catch this graceful display of the Self.

(5) However, at the same time, the I-thought or I-am-the-body idea is jumping from the sleep/dream station to the waking state station. This "I am the body" thought, even though it is the source of the mind, cannot last for very long if it does not have a body or station to claim as it own, as its (false) identity.

(6) This I-thought is no slouch. It moves VERY quickly. You may notice that it is moving up from the Heart on the right (right side of the chest) to the head.

(7) As you experience success with this special effortless Morning Meditation, the GAP will get bigger and brighter. Eventually, this spaciousness and lightness of being will begin to permeate your daily life.

At some point, it becomes clear to you that you are the Self, the World is the Self, and everything is the Self. There is only the Self. Once you are established and stabilized in this understanding, you have attained full spiritual enlightenment.

(8) You are also encouraged to do at least 20 minutes of sitting "Who am I?" (Self-inquiry) meditation every day. The format for doing this meditation is to notice when thoughts rise up. I have called it the "practical two-step" meditation.

When a thought rises up you ask "Who is having this thought?" The thought will answer "I am." This answer is coming from the I-am-the-body thought.

The second step or question that you ask is "Where did you come from?" Since this I-thought came from the Heart or the causal source, and it is not your true identity, it has been exposed for the sham that it is. So it retreats, ashamed so to speak, the winds taken from its sails, back down into its source (the Heart).

(9) During the day when you are going to and from work, or any other "stealth" opportunity, such as at lunch while at work, you "steal" a few minutes to do the two-step Self-inquiry meditation and challenge any thoughts that are arising.

If these thoughts are about people or things in the world around you, that is just fine. It doesn't matter what the content of the thoughts may be. Every thought is ultimately about being the body and the ramifications for you of that. Every thought can be traced back to the original thought which is "I am the body."

(10) If you can also follow the transition at night from waking state to sleep/dream state that is good, but it is not necessary. When doing deep meditation, the most important thing is to get good sleep. Do NOT interfere with the deep sleep state!

WHERE DO YOU GO FROM HERE?

What you have learned in this course is the essence of Self-inquiry or "Who am I?" meditation. It is explained like this in such a plain and straightforward way. I believe that the world is ready for such direct explanations and step by step instructions, so I have provided them.

The next section of this course is the Recommended Reading list, which has all of my favorite Self-inquiry resources that have helped me so much. The final section of the course is information on how to contact me if you are interested in further study with this approach to Self-inquiry and "Who am I?" meditation.

The fact that I am making myself available is not a statement that you need me in order to do this practice. Quite the contrary! You are already the Self!

However, if your inner guidance system prompts you to contact me, then I would say that you should follow it. Although the Self is everywhere, it just seems that the way things work in life is that some circumstances, such as having a spiritual teacher or at least consulting with one, are more favorable and can be of real help.

It may be getting just one critical question answered, or it may be a lot more, but since we are all human beings, we tend to do better when we can get constructive help from someone who has already walked this path that we are walking on now.

The teacher does not give freedom to the student. The student is already free. The genuine teacher knows and sees without effort that the student is already enlightened and is already the Self. Such as teacher sees only enlightenment or the Self everywhere. So it is automatic to see the student that way, too.

What the teacher does is help the student eliminate the false mental confusion that was blinding him or her from the reality of who and what they are -- the Self, the primal Awareness, the Light of Reality. In fact, it is only the student who can do this work. The teacher can help in mysterious ways, but the student saves himself.

RECOMMENDED READING

For a better understanding of the scientific view of the stages of sleep at night, I found this wiki article to be quite useful: http://en.wikipedia.org/wiki/Sleep

One of the most complete resources for books about the teachings of Sri Ramana Maharshi by Ramana Maharshi himself and other qualified teachers is the AHAM web site. It is impressive as they have just about everything, no matter how rare. They also offer training programs in their own unique approach to Self-inquiry.

http://www.aham.com/usa/bookstore/bhagavan_suggested.html

In the case of the web sites of Michael James and David Godman, referenced below, you have Westerners who are experts on Ramana's words and translations.

On this AHAM Books page is the physical book by Sri Sadhu Om from India that I referred to several times in this book: *The Path of Sri Ramana, Part One*. Part One is about Self-inquiry. Part Two is about surrender and devotion (bhakti).

While you can purchase the physical book from AHAM at the online address above, you also have the option to download the free pdf ebook version of Sri Sadhu Om's "The Path of Sri Ramana, Part One" at the web site of Michael James.

The extraordinary value of this little book for the student of "Who am I?" meditation and Self-inquiry is unparallelled.

Sri Sadhu Om has "spilled the beans," so to speak, removing all the confusing esoteric stuff to reveal the pure practical essence. What is left is a V-8 engine of meditation that works.

Since Michael James was deeply involved in the translation and publication through various editions of this book over the years, there is no impropriety here. In fact, in the pdf it shows that the copyright of this translation is in his name.

He is generously offering it for free download with full consent of the book's publisher. He also has a web page where books can be purchased.

http://www.happinessofbeing.com/The_Path_of_Sri_Ramana_Part_One.pdf

http://www.happinessofbeing.com/path_ramana.html

http://www.happinessofbeing.com/books.html

The above web page provides a handy summary and overview of both Part One and Part Two. Michael is an excellent writer with deep objective insights.

On other pages of this web site, he explores fine points of Sri Sadhu Om's method. As the late Sri Sadhu Om Swamigal's friend and translator, he is qualified to provide original insights, including those obtained via private conversations. I am calling it Sri Sadhu Om's method, but what it really is is the method of Sri Ramana Maharshi elucidated to ultimate transparency for the sake of practical application.

http://happinessofbeing.blogspot.com/2011/01/second-and-third-person-objects.html

http://happinessofbeing.blogspot.com/2007/08/atma-vichara-and-question-who-am-i.html

http://happinessofbeing.blogspot.com/2007/08/question-who-am-i-as-verbalised-thought.html

Like Michael James, David Godman has spent many years living in India near the blessed Mount Arunachala where Sri Ramana Maharshi provided his grace and teachings. To appreciate the depth at which David writes, here is a web page that deals with "Aham Sphurana." You can search the Internet and elsewhere, you will not find a more lucid exposition of this difficult and abstruse subject.

http://davidgodman.org/rteach/iandii1.shtml

In short, if you want to learn more about the teachings of Sri Ramana Maharshi, David's website should be on your short list. He also sells books on his site.

In my opinion, many of the writers seeking to make public the teachings of Sri Ramana Maharshi did not themselves have a profound grasp of Self-inquiry. As a result, their presentation of it can be confusing at best.

The late sage Annamalai Swami spent 10 years with Sri Ramana Maharshi. His down to earth teachings on Self-realization, based on the transmission he received directly from Ramana, are a reliable guide to Ramana's message.

His very practical teachings can be found in *Annamalai Swami: Final Talks*. He is also author of an illuminating autobiography called *Living By the Words of Bhagavan*.

Both are published by the AHAM Publications, Asheboro, SC, USA cited above. AHAM is the place in the USA to get books related to Sri Ramana Maharshi. A. Ramana, AHAM'S late guru, expresses the Heart beautifully in his books. He reveals much about the experience of the Heart in them.

Last but not least is a profound guide to Self-inquiry and the true nature of the I-thought called *No Mind, I Am the Self*. Edited by David Godman, it is the words of Sri Lakshmana Swamy, one of the last living students of Sri Ramana as well as an enlightened recipient of his Grace.

It goes into detail about the spiritual journey of his enlightened disciple Mathru Sri Sarada Ma and the relationship between the guru and the disciple. It also explains the role of meditation and the thought-free state in this sadhana. This book is highly recommended!

Note: A different form of inquiry in the form of four questions is offered by Byron Katie. I recommend her method also. For more information, you can go to her website TheWork.com.

Her bestselling book is *Loving What Is*. Beyond the method itself, I would say the real benefit of her message is a clear perspective on thoughts: Do NOT believe your thoughts! If you look at her four questions plus a turnaround from the point of view of classical Self-inquiry, you will see it is a brilliant adaptation. You can use it thought by thought or embrace the big picture: the mind is just making stuff up!

Meet the Author

RAMAJI

Ramaji teaches Advaita and non-duality in the San Diego, California area. He has been a devotee of Kali Ma since She spoke to him at the Hollywood Vedanta Society Temple in 1982. He is easily reached via email or his web site Ramaji.org.

Ramaji works with students all over the world via email and Skype. He currently has students in Australia, Thailand, United Kingdom, Brazil, Japan, India, Canada and the United States.

Although there is a small fee for the RASA transmission, the personal spiritual coaching and ongoing non-dual dialog he provides to his students is offered on a love donation basis.

He teaches Self-inquiry in the tradition of Ramana Maharshi with a non-dual Tantra and Kundalini twist. Ultimately, the essence of inquiry is passion for Truth, whatever the form.

His work includes guiding students in the investigation of the arising I-thought, stabilization in the thought-free state, revelation of the Heart on the right and illumination of the Amrita Nadi.

Ramaji also provides support for people on a devotional path with Divine Mother, Kali Ma devotees especially, and for awakening Kundalini experiencers.

Via telephone, Skype or in person, he offers RASA (Ramaji Advaita Satsang Attunement). This attunement into non-dual consciousness opens the Crown chakra to Divine Mother's gentle descending Grace for rapid awakening of enlightenment. Some experience this radiant spiritual download as a white or golden light.

As the Crown chakra opens, identification with the physical body is reduced. A brightly glowing wide open Crown chakra is one of the characteristics of an enlightened person. It is a sign that body identification has been dropped.

Many Blessings in the One Supreme Self,
RAMAJI

Ramaji.org

Meetup.com/Ramaji-Satsang-Group/ (local San Diego meetings)

YouTube Channel: Ramaji Satsang

Email: satsangwithramaji@gmail.com

Waking Up As Awareness

Made in the USA
Lexington, KY
05 November 2016